Jeannette Klute

Jeannette Klute

A PHOTOGRAPHIC PIONEER

Therese Mulligan

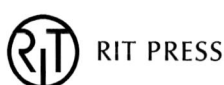 RIT PRESS

Rochester, New York

RIT Press
90 Lomb Memorial Drive
Rochester, New York 14623-5604
http://ritpress.rit.edu

Book design by Marnie Soom
Cover photo: Photographer Unknown, Portrait of Jeannette Klute, ca. 1950.
Photograph courtesy of Nancy Pease.
Printed in the U.S.A.
ISBN 978-1-939125-43-9

All works are by Jeannette Klute (American, b. 1918, Rochester, NY, d. 2009, South Bristol, NY)
and appear courtesy of the Rochester Institute of Technology's Archive Collections,
unless otherwise noted. All photographs are Dye Transfer prints, with exceptions noted.

Library of Congress Cataloging-in-Publication Data

Names: Mulligan, Therese, author. Simmons, Becky, writer of introduction.
    | Klute, Jeannette, 1918–2009 Photographs Selections. | Rochester Institute of Technology, issuing body.
Title: Jeannette Klute, a photographic pioneer / [text by] Therese Mulligan.
Other titles: Photographic pioneer
Description: Rochester, New York : RIT Press, [2017] | Includes
    bibliographical references.
Identifiers: LCCN 2017013779 (print) | LCCN 2017017231 (ebook) | ISBN
    9781939125446 (ebook) | ISBN 9781939125439 (print (softcover) : alk.
    paper) | ISBN 9781939125446 (e-book)
Subjects: LCSH: Nature photography. | Color photography—Printing
    processes—Dye transfer. | Klute, Jeannette, 1918–2009 | Photographers—United
    States—Biography.
Classification: LCC TR721 (ebook) | LCC TR721 .J43 2017 (print) | DDC
    778.9/3—dc23
LC record available at https://lccn.loc.gov/2017013779

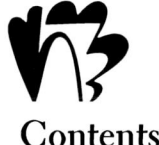

Contents

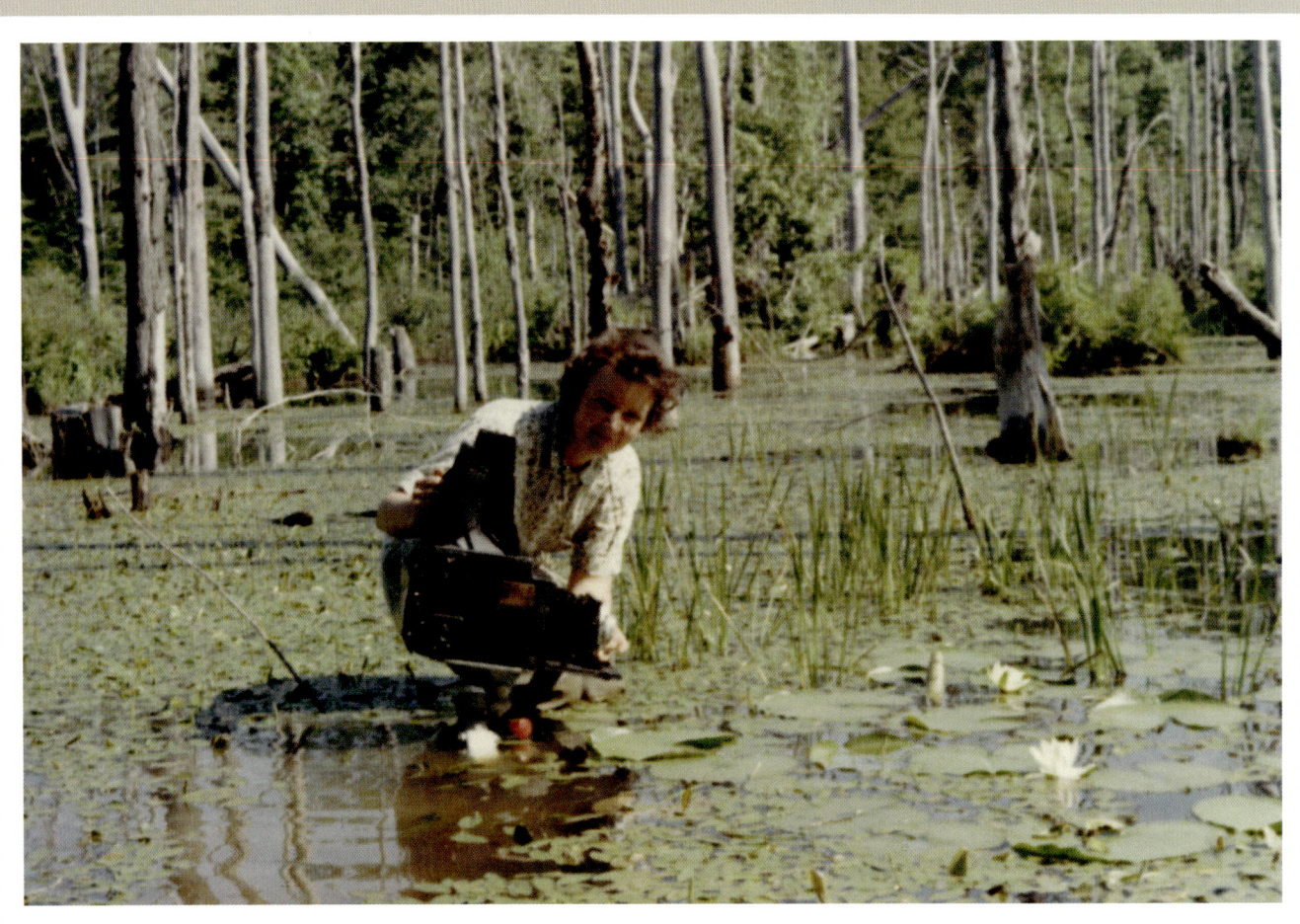

Jeannette Klute with Graflex Camera, ca. 1950

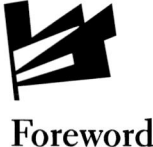

Foreword

RIT Libraries and RIT Archive Collections are pleased to introduce the first title in a new series of chapbooks celebrating RIT's rich history and the unique holdings preserved in the department. Chapbooks originated in the 16th century, as heavily illustrated paperback booklets, with a short accompanying literary or didactic text. Produced and printed inexpensively, they were intended for those who were unable to afford a full-length book. The format and sensibility of this new series adopts this tradition, and will feature an essay accompanied by illustrations that are obtained from the Archives. The series will feature stories of influential people, key events, themes related to education and the curriculum, as well as other subjects connected to RIT's history. We hope to offer the RIT community and beyond, an opportunity to better understand the depth and breadth of the collections.

Housed in The Wallace Center at RIT, with a mission to acquire, preserve, and make the holdings accessible, RIT Archive Collections includes four main areas of focus: RIT Archives, RIT Art Collection, RIT/NTID Deaf Studies Archive, and Special Collections. RIT Archives serves as the official repository for university records with historical, administrative and legal value, including minutes of major governance groups, departmental records, and reports and papers of the presidents. Dating back to the founding of RIT in 1829, RIT Archives include hundreds of thousands of photographs, official and student publications, news clippings, videos and audio tapes of programs and events, oral history interviews, posters, architectural drawings, and numerous artifacts and ephemera. The Archives provide an institutional memory, ensuring that a well-rounded view of RIT's unique history, from major decisions by the trustees to student events, has adequate documentation. The associated RIT Art Collection relates directly to the school's rich history of visual arts education that began in 1886 with classes in clay modeling, painting, and design. Hundreds of fine, finished works created by faculty, students, and alumni, attest to the talent of the individuals as well as to the shifts in style and taste over time. Numerous examples of classroom exercises illustrate the historical range of RIT's art programs which showcase trends in art education. The entire art collection has an important educational component, offering RIT students an opportunity to experience visual art directly, and see works in their chosen field, providing a historical context for their learning. The art collections have grown tremendously in recent years, with significant acquisitions of groups of works by individual artists, including ceramic works by School for American Crafts instructor Frans Wildenhain, and Jeannette Klute's photographic work, the subject of this book.

In 1965, RIT was chosen as the home of the newly established National Technical Institute for the Deaf (NTID). A third major archive collection, the RIT/NTID Deaf Studies Archive, documents NTID's vital role in educating the deaf and hard of hearing, and the important research in the field undertaken by faculty and staff. Drawing from sources within Rochester's deaf community, as well as around the nation, the archives include: Deaf culture, education, theater, artistic expression, poetry, and literature and the development of technologies for the deaf. Special Collections, including the business and personal papers of Rochester businessman and philanthropist B. Thomas Golisano, and sizeable holdings of 20th-century editorial cartoons, round out the Archives's primary holdings. Together, the archive collections document the tremendous growth of the institution and RIT's 188 years as a significant contributor to the Rochester and upstate New York communities. Topics as diverse as RIT's first president, to the growth of the downtown campus to apparatus fabricated and used by a student in an early 20th century mechanical arts class, offer examples of the countless subjects that can be explored within the chapbook series.

This chapbook highlights the Jeannette Klute Collection of photographs and personal papers. Klute attended RIT in the 1940s, but left her studies after she was hired to work at Eastman Kodak. At the company, she rose to become research photographer in charge of the Visual Research Studio of the Color Technology Division. She also became an expert in the Dye Transfer process, and her photographic work forms the core of the Jeannette Klute Collection. Generously donated by Klute's longtime friend, Nancy Pease, the Jeannette Klute Collection includes over one hundred of Klute's large-format, color saturated, Dye Transfer prints of native plants, animals, and tide-pool scenes as well as an example of the unique Derivation process that she co-developed. Six boxes of personal papers document her career and her photographic work, including correspondence, articles and clippings about Klute, print files, records of exhibitions and sales, subject files, and artifacts, including field logs. Much of Ms. Klute's life story can be gleaned from these files, and the University is indeed privileged to have been entrusted with this important collection.

Archives speak to context, and every collection has fascinating links and associations to the circumstances surrounding the creation of the records. The Jeannette Klute Collection is no exception. Her life and work is intertwined with RIT's role in photographic education, the Eastman Kodak Company during its heyday, the company's role in the development of color photography and the Dye Transfer process, and the rise of color photography as an art form. There are also more personal associations from Ms. Klute's focus on indigenous plants and landscape, and her deep appreciation of the area around Honeoye Lake, where she made her home and photographed for so many years. Her photographs will continue to bear witness to the beauty of the Finger Lakes. She also helped found and took part in the Naples Open Studio Trail for many years, opening up her home and giving visitors from near and far a chance to share her passion for photography and the land. The Jeannette Klute Collection and the chapbook will provide a lasting legacy for this important local artist, dedicated employee, and contributor to the community.

I must acknowledge my good friend and colleague Therese Mulligan, Administrative Chair of the School of Photographic Arts and Sciences at RIT. A photo historian, she conducted extensive research into Jeannette Klute's work and career, and wrote the essay that examines Klute's work against the backdrop of the academic history of photography. We worked together on this chapbook and organized the exhibition of Klute's work in the Photo School's William Harris Gallery in fall 2017. I salute her knowledge of photographic history, experience with exhibitions, management skills, and attention to detail. Without Therese, this project would not have happened.

Becky Simmons
RIT Archivist

Acknowledgments

Many hands, minds, and hearts go into the making of a publication. The authors would like to thank the individuals who supported this book since its inception, and provided invaluable assistance in its final production. We are grateful for the opportunity to visit with Nancy Pease and Beth Lyons. As close friends of Jeannette Klute, they spent an afternoon bringing us closer to the photographer's life, career, and artistic work. We couldn't be more appreciative of their help with this book project. Thanks especially to Ms. Pease. As Ms. Klute's executor, she donated the collection of Klute images now housed in the RIT Archives Collections. The collection is of great benefit to the educational mission and goals of the Archives, and will enlighten faculty, students, alumni, and an interested public about a critical moment in modern color photography for generations to come. This book is dedicated to her and to the indomitable spirit, career, and photographic art of Jeannette Klute.

The authors thank Eastman Kodak Company, and its representative Laura Zigarowicz, for permission to reproduce photographs created by Klute for company products and instruction.

The authors would also like to give a special acknowledgement to Lauren Alberque for her exceptionally clear explanation of the Dye Transfer and the Derivation processes.

Special acknowledgment to the RIT Press for their long advocacy of this project, from concept to realization. The authors are indebted to Press Director, Bruce Austin; Managing Editor, Molly Cort; and Designer, Marnie Soom for their expertise and generous support.

The RIT Archives staff and student employees were indispensable colleagues in the shaping of this publication. They catalogued and housed the Klute collection, gathering important information about the photographer as well as individual and group photographs, so to enable accessibility to the collection by student and scholar alike.

An allied purpose of this book is to create a permanent record of an exhibition of the Klute collection on display in the William Harris Gallery in 2017. The William Harris Gallery is located in the School of Photographic Arts and Sciences, and supports photo-related exhibitions, events, and speakers. It works actively with the RIT Archives to present important collected work and/or individual artists, especially RIT alumni, for the educational advancement of the Gallery and School's mission.

Finally, the authors are appreciative of family and friends, in particular John Rudy and Betsy and Rick Saxe, for their steadfast companionship throughout the journey to realize this publication and associated exhibition.

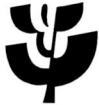

Living Color: The Photography of Jeannette Klute

On most Fridays in 1938, Jeannette Klute (1918–2009) visited the personnel office of Eastman Kodak Company in search of employment. Yet, each time, she was turned away. Klute was twenty years old and had spent the year enrolled in the Mechanics' Institute, then located in downtown Rochester, NY. When she enrolled in the Mechanics' Institute, it was during the closing years of the Great Depression (fig. 1). Jobs were still scarce — even in a company town such as Rochester — and technical or trade programs pointed a new path to skilled jobs and, hopefully, financial security. For Klute, as for other Rochester residents, Kodak represented a singular hometown company for possible employment: "The word was that Kodak was the place to work, so I thought…why don't I take photography and get a job at Kodak. Nothing to it."[1] But securing a position at Kodak, especially if one was a woman, was anything but easy. That was until October of 1938 when a personnel director, worn down by Klute's persistence, finally gave her a position as a photography technician developing exposed film. For the next forty-three years, she worked at Kodak, enlarging her role far beyond that of a lab technician. Klute's career would intersect with the company's authoritative status in the popular development of modern color photography in the 1940s and 1950s and then later, in the 1970s, the re-discovery of pioneering women photographers by feminist counterparts involved in the women's movement.

The Mechanics' Institute's mission fulfilled the instructional purpose of similar education centers situated around the world: providing access to

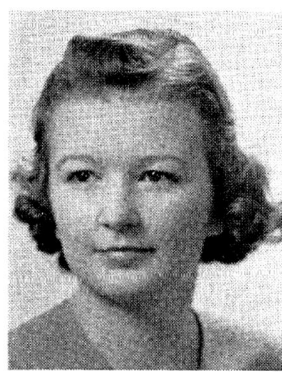

KLUTE, J.

1. Jeannette Klute's yearbook picture from Mechanics' Institute, 1939.

scientific and technological training for the working class, primarily made up of men, in preparation to enter industry. This gender preference was not lost on Klute when she arrived for her first day of classes. Her class consisted of forty men and three women, including Klute. The Institute had a strong cooperative education component: classroom training and on-the-job training went hand in hand to create a skilled and knowledgeable employee. With no prior photography experience and her vocational aspirations set on Kodak, Klute took classes in the Photographic Technology department. Founded in 1930 as the economic crisis of the Great Depression took hold in the United States, it was supported by Rochester's many photography-aligned industries. The goal of the department was to prepare students for a variety of photographic careers: professional photography, photographic services, and manufacturing or selling of photographic equipment and supplies (fig. 2). The students were involved in an intensive curriculum, with courses ranging from photographic skills, chemistry, physics, and retouching, to photographic materials and processes. (The latter class has been taught continuously since 1930. In 1944, the Institute adopted the name Rochester Institute of Technology [RIT] and the photography department evolved into a comprehensive school incorporating the photographic arts and photographic sciences.) With an acumen for hard work, unbridled self-confidence, and ambition, Klute wasted little time during her first year of coursework applying for a position at Kodak, even though she was told by Institute officials that few women were ever selected for employment. Her personal strengths and abilities would define much of what she would accomplish in her diverse career as both a longtime Kodak employee and a creative photographer.

Once Klute went through the doors at Kodak, her involvement with the Mechanics' Institute lessened, but did not end, even when her work provided ample opportunity for professional training. She remained a student in the Photography program through 1939. Looking for new assignments in the company beyond her initial tasks as a lab assistant — one of the few positions held by women besides receptionist — Klute took Saturday classes in 1944 at the newly named Rochester Institute of Technology, in

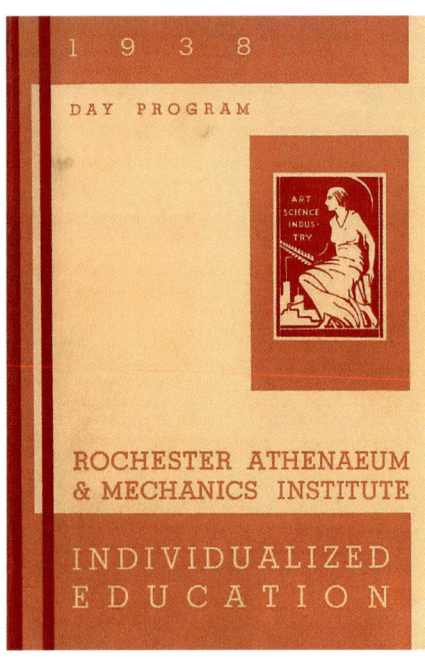

2. Cover of Mechanics' Institute catalogue, 1938.

advanced photographic technologies, more significantly color processes.[2] She built her repertoire of skills and in 1945, she was named head of the color printing group, and by 1949, was a research photographer in charge of the Visual Research Studio of the Color Technology Division. In these new positions, she emerged as a highly regarded photographer, whose duties included testing, improving, and illustrating the reproduction of color material and processes. In the mid-1940s, the newest in color technology was the introduction and professional reception of Dye Transfer printing.

Color photography as embraced by the mass-market and professional photographers had long been the aim of Kodak, beginning with its founder George Eastman, who, in 1914, trademarked and exhibited an early version of the Kodachrome color process for the amateur market. Strides in color technology were many in the first half of the twentieth century. In 1936, Kodak launched its perfected Kodachrome process, for seventy years the company's most popular transparency roll film for amateur and professional photographer alike until its discontinuance in 2009 with the rise of digital image capture technology. During World War II, Kodak, like other industries, turned much of its resources to supporting the war effort, but it introduced new color products. These included Minicolor printing (1941) and Kodacolor film (1942). With the end of the war, Kodak, having generated a heightened public demand for color photography with its products, rapidly promoted recently developed technologies. In 1945, the Dye Transfer printing process was rolled out with an eye to the professional market. With an origin in the motion picture industry, the Dye Transfer process was known by other names, including dye imbibition printing and wash-off relief printing, during phases of its development. The process represented a leap forward in photographic printing innovation due to its stability, continuous tone, and a reliable fidelity of the color spectrum. For the professional photographer, the Dye Transfer process required technical knowledge and handwork similar to that undertaken by a printmaker. The exacting and labor-intensive process offered unparalleled control of all facets of the printing process, including color hues, tonal gradation, and contrast. (A thorough description of the Dye Transfer printing process can be found on p. 21.)

In development and refinement, Klute played a key role in Dye Transfer printing technology in particular, and color photography, such as Kodachrome, in general. Her central position as a research photographer of color processes and materials can be attributed not only to her own ambitions as a photographer, but to her working relationship with Kodak scientist, Ralph M. Evans, a world authority in the disciplines of color and vision. Within two years of arriving at Kodak, Klute was invited by Evans, then head of color development and quality control in Kodak laboratories, to provide illustrations for his slide lectures, articles, and books. She would work closely with Evans until his retirement in 1971.

A 1929 graduate of the Massachusetts Institute of Technology, Evans trained in physics, maintaining a strong interest in color science and photography. At Kodak (1928, 1935–1971), in addition to supervising the development of color processes, he took up the study of the phenomena of color and vision. Evans' first book, *An Introduction to Color*, published in 1948, is regarded today as a classic text on modern color science, attentive to the physiological and psychological implications of color in photography. Herbert Kalmus, acclaimed color scientist and president of the Technicolor Motion Picture Corporation, wrote in a 1949 review that the book was a "must for the artist, technician, and scientist in color and related arts."[3]

Evans described complex technical or theoretical concepts with the persuasive use of accessible, well-composed illustrations in his books. In *An Introduction to Color*, Klute's black and white and color photographs, reproduced from original Dye Transfer images produced in Evans' lab, share pages with detailed graphic presentations of scientific representations. Whether photographic or diagrammatic, illustrations served as a further example or elucidation to deepen the weight of Evans' written perspective. An instance of this is Plate V in *An Introduction to Color Photography* (fig. 3), where Klute illustrates how, as the accompanying caption describes, the "perception of depth is affected by the lighting contrast of a scene."

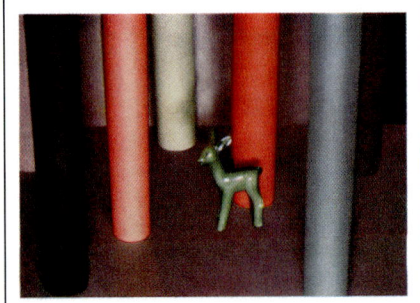

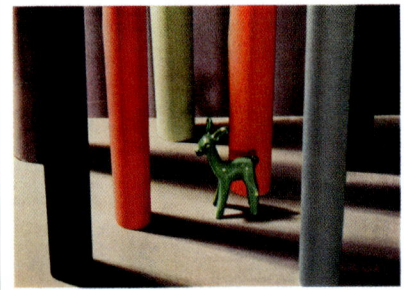

PLATE V

The perception of depth is affected by the lighting contrast of the scene. The upper scene has diffuse front lighting. The identical scene, with non-diffuse high-contrast side lighting (*below*), gives a much greater perception of depth.

3. Plate V from *An Introduction to Color* by Ralph M. Evans, 1948. This plate describes how "perception of depth is affected by the lighting contrast of a scene." Illustration by Jeannette Klute.

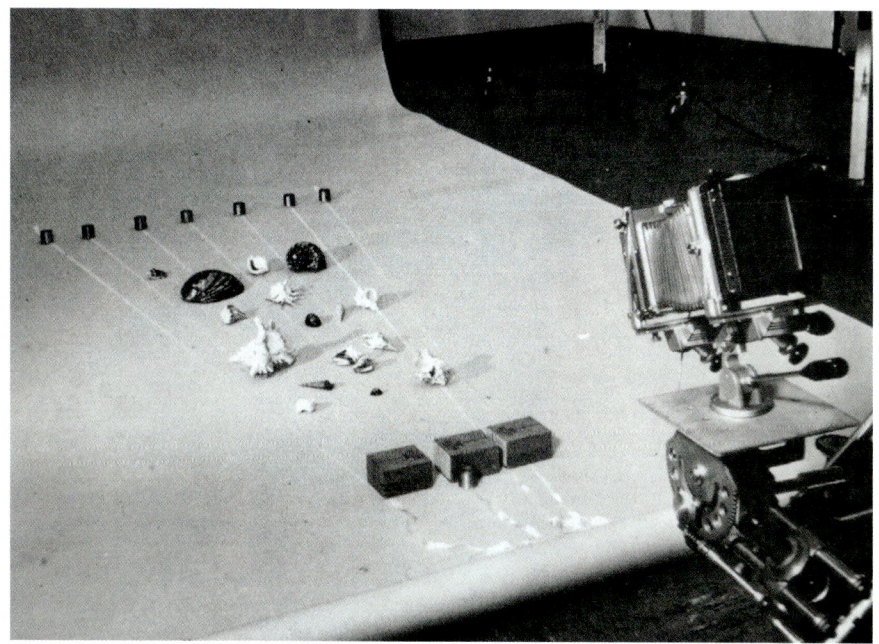

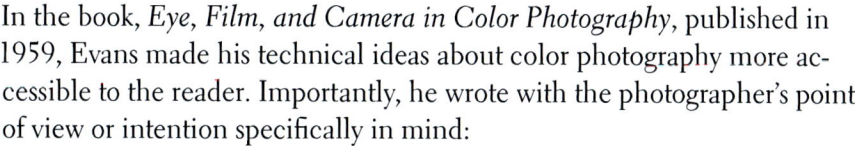

4. Illustration on perspective and convergence by Jeannette Klute in Ralph M. Evans' book *Eye, Film, And Camera in Color Photography*, 1959, p. 273.

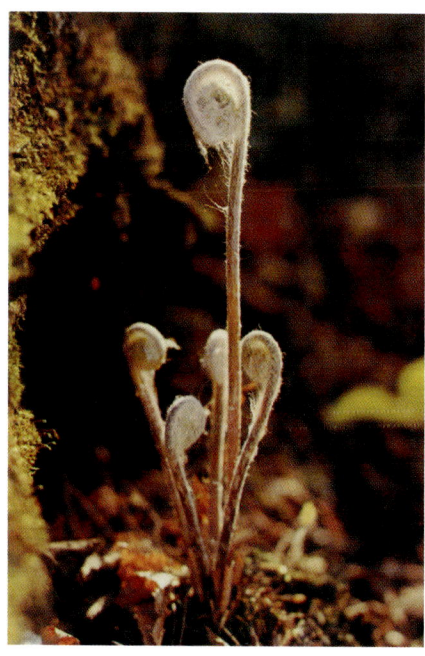

5. This image by Klute of a back-lighted Cinnamon fern, held in the RIT Archives Collections, appeared as a color illustration in the book *Eye, Film, and Camera in Color Photography*, 1959.

In the book, *Eye, Film, and Camera in Color Photography*, published in 1959, Evans made his technical ideas about color photography more accessible to the reader. Importantly, he wrote with the photographer's point of view or intention specifically in mind:

> What an observer sees when he looks at a scene, can be and usually is very different from what he sees when he is looking at an 'accurate' color photograph of that scene. The contents of this book are the result of twenty years of continuing investigation into this difference in its various aspects. This has been done both to learn what the differences are and to find out how the photographer may either offset them or make use of them for his particular purposes.[4]

As in Evans' earlier book, Klute's images dominate: "It is a real pleasure to acknowledge the direct assistance of those who have helped in the production of this book. Miss Jeannette Klute, who over the years has made all the photographs for my lectures, is again responsible for all the photographs in this book."[5] While illustrative pictures, typically black and white reproductions describing technical concepts are in abundance in this book, such as the image describing the concept of perspective and convergence to be seen through Klute's featured camera (fig. 4), other images, including color plates, draw upon Klute's own creative photographic preoccupations: nature photographs (fig. 5) and experimental color photographs known as *Derivations* (fig. 6). In *Eye, Film and Camera in Color Photography*, it would be Klute's distinctive images that distinguished for Evans and his readers how a color photograph in the hands of a professional photographer with creative aspirations would incorporate intent, technique, and style for 'particular purposes'.

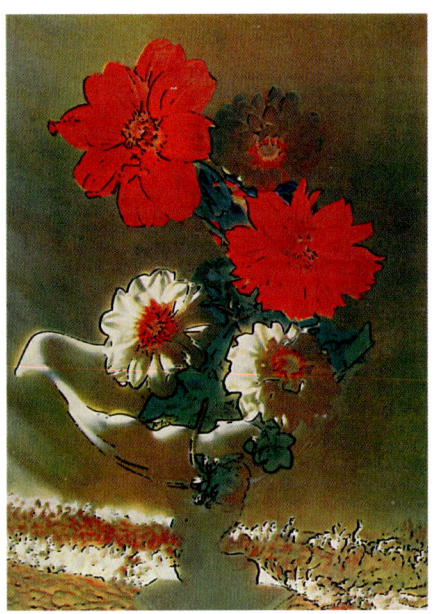

6. *Derivation*, 1951. Used with permission from Eastman Kodak Company.

Evans was certainly one of the first of Klute's colleagues to notice her artistic inclinations early on in her career. His authority in photography lent an important stamp of legitimacy and recommendation: "As director of her work since 1940 I have had a good opportunity to watch her unique ability develop."[6] He further noted: "[Her] work has run the gamut of photographic requirements, from explicit representation of objects in detail to pictures showing the application of photographic theory to artistic ends."[7] In her artistic color photographic work, Klute concentrated visually on two different realms where she felt most at home: the natural landscape (fig 7) and the color laboratory at Kodak.

WOODLAND PORTRAITS
In 1954, Klute published her one and only monograph, *Woodland Portraits*. This volume of 50 color plates, derived from Dye Transfer prints produced by the staff in Klute's color laboratory, celebrated the flora and fauna of woodlands found right outside her home's back door and at a nearby swamp in South Bristol, located southeast of Rochester in the Finger Lakes region (fig. 8). For Klute, the natural landscape was as central

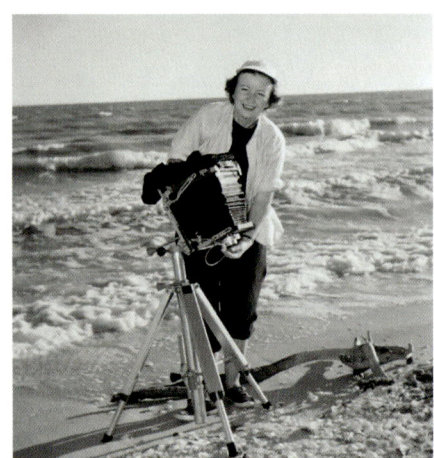

7. Portrait of Klute at work in the field. She often used her white hat as a light reflector. From the collection of Nancy Pease.

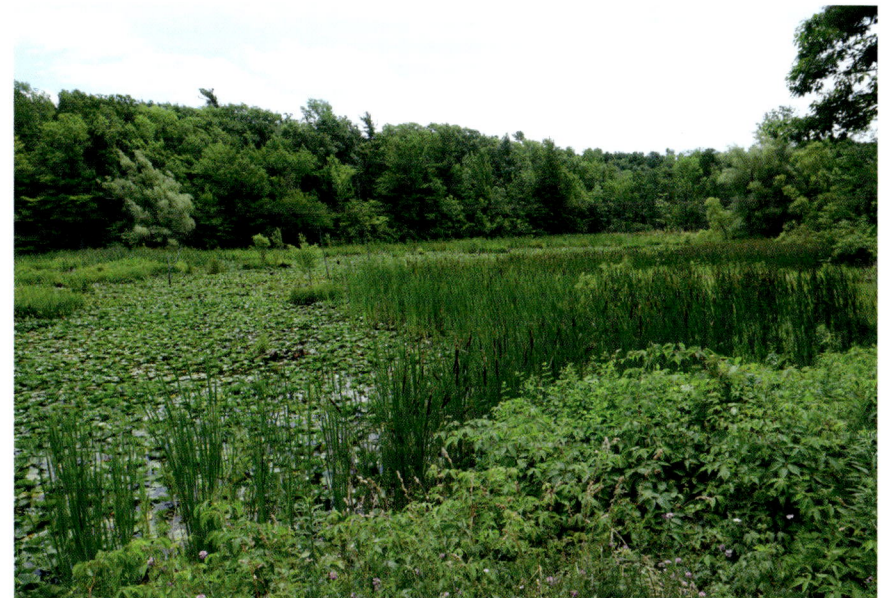

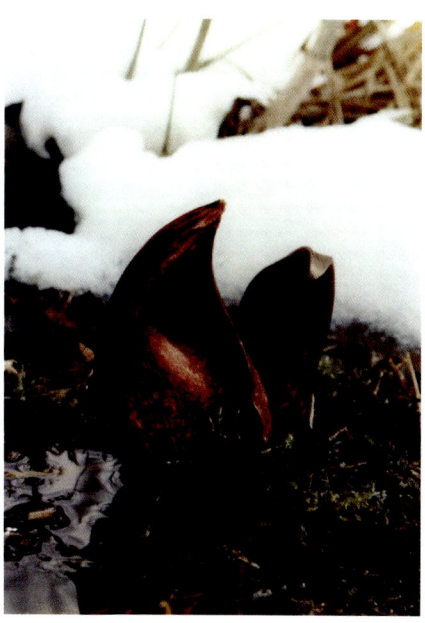

8. Klute found a majority of her subjects for *Woodland Portraits* around the pond located behind her home in South Bristol, NY. Photo courtesy of Therese Mulligan.

9. *Skunk-cabbage*, Plate 1, from *Woodland Portraits*.

to her life as it was to her work as a photographer. This is elucidated when she describes the motivation behind *Woodland Portraits*:

> My purpose has been to somehow express the feeling one experiences being out of doors. I am concerned with the delight to the senses as much as with the intellectual. The woods are mystical and enchanting to me as well as spiritual.[8]

To accentuate the "mystical and spiritual" or simply the mood of the pictured natural detail, Klute arranged her images into three seasonal groups; "Spring; Summer: June and July; and Late Summer and Autumn." Significantly, she also appended poetry she selected to her images, as seen in Plate 1, *Skunk-cabbage*, (fig. 9) with text by the English poet and playwright, Alfred Noyes: "…And what d'you suppose is that other faint sound — Snow melting? — leaves budding? — or young lovers whispering all round…?[9]

Five years earlier, in the book *Eye, Film and Camera in Color Photography*, Evans spoke to the combined use of words and pictures: "Taken together and properly used, words and pictures are the most powerful means of communication known to us. However presented they will convey some sort of idea powerfully."[10] Certainly, it can be inferred that Evans was referring to the picture press in which images are combined with descriptive captions to tell a story. He was knowledgeable of the history of photography in which creative photographers used text to elevate the imaginative and expressive ideas expounded in their work. For Klute, it was her understanding of the lineage of art photography and art history, and her considered placement of word and image that sought to prompt an awareness or emotional response to the special forces at work in nature. To further emphasize the expressive nature of her work, Klute purposefully chose a selective lens focus with a shallow depth of field when picturing natural subjects.

In the Photographic Appendix to *Woodland Portraits*, Klute specifies technical information pertaining to each of the color plates presented in her monograph. She includes such information as date, camera, lens, film, settings, and length of exposure, the day's light conditions — cloudy, sunny, overcast — and personal remarks relevant to color and its effects on a subject, camera positions, or what she experienced in the act of photographing (fig. 10). Such published details, not commonplace in art photography today, were not unusual at this phase in the development of modern photography. The technical aspects of the medium and the maker's control

PLATE 1

Skunk-cabbage
QUOTATION FROM: "The Last of the Snow," by Alfred Noyes
DATE: March 11
CAMERA: Auto Graflex, 4 x 5
LENS: 8½" Kodak Anastigmat
FILM: Ektachrome
EXPOSURE: f/32 5 sec. CC-15 filter
DAY: Hazy overcast
REMARKS: The range in brightness values offered a challenge here. The aim was to keep snow looking like snow, with as much detail as possible—and then to put detail in the shadow area on the inside of the skunk-cabbage. This is even more of a challenge when making a print, since the range is shorter than that of a color transparency. The day was hazy and overcast, which kept down the brilliance of the snow; and a reflector was used for the shadows. The reflector used was a white sheet and also a small mirror.

10. Page from Klute's *Woodland Portraits* discussing technical information per photographed image.

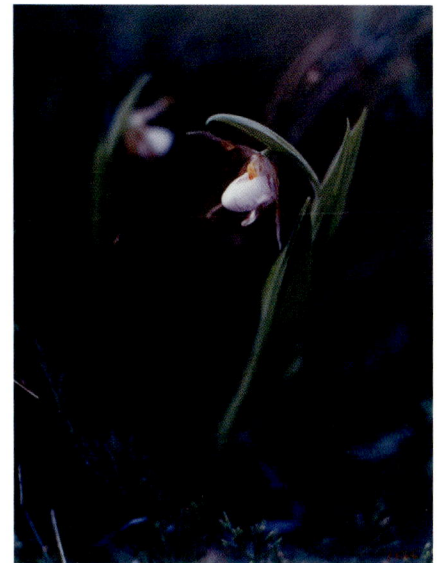

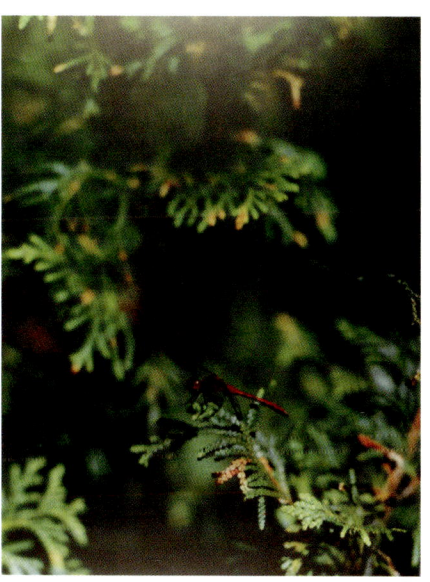

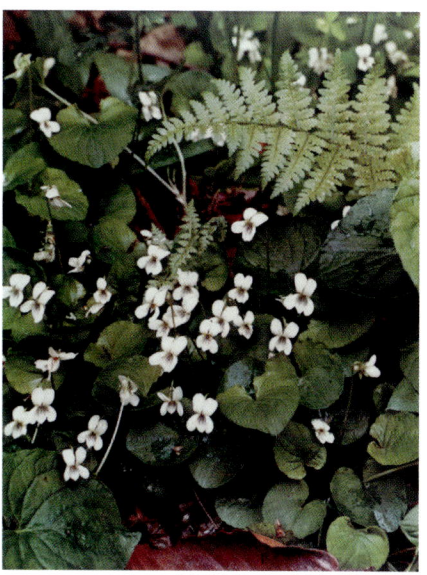

11. Small White Lady's-slipper, Plate 16, from *Woodland Portraits*.

12. Red-tailed Dragonfly on White Cedar, Plate 32, from *Woodland Portraits*.

13. White Violet, Plate 21, from *Woodland Portraits*.

of these aspects was highly prized as part of the essence of a finished photograph. Klute's professional occupation as a research photographer, required her to demonstrate the technology supporting accurate color photographs as they related directly to a captured subject or view, and as an art photographer for whom mastery of her medium and its inherent materials and processes was considered a paramount responsibility. Such was the consequence of much modern photography in the 1940s and 1950s and as seen in the landscape works of Ansel Adams, Edward Weston, and fellow color landscape photographer, Elliot Porter.

In *Woodland Portraits*, Klute's mastery of the color medium was infused with evocation and beauty. Her intentional selection of a shallow depth of field for a close-up view, with an out-of-focus background enabled her to highlight the fine lyrical line of a flower (fig. 11), the graceful agility of an insect alighted on a branch (fig. 12), or the colorful display of a quiet riot of petals and stems (fig. 13). The pictorial effect is painterly, characterized by intense and saturated color, enhanced surface textures and the revealing essence of light. All of these elements, including the addition of poetic verse, gave voice to the aesthetic qualities Klute hoped to instill in her nature photography, as well as to the mystery and spirit she looked to communicate about the woodlands. They also demonstrated the artistic possibilities of new color photographic techniques for the modern art photographer, grounded in the predominant black and white picture aesthetic of the day. Upon receiving *Woodland Portraits*, acclaimed photographer Ansel Adams wrote to the publisher: "I think Miss Klute has made a major contribution to creative photography — a new and fresh approach, and avoidance of the sterile color and moods of the greater part of contemporary color photography."[11]

Klute's nature photographs, including those found in *Woodland Portraits*, were on display when photographers toured Kodak facilities to view what was new in photographic technology. Significant practitioners and museum curators, such as Ansel Adams, Minor White, Margaret Bourke-White, and Beaumont Newhall, George Eastman House's first photography curator, visited the Visual Research Studio, led by Ralph Evans, and came into contact with Klute's work. It was pronounced a leading representative of the expressive possibilities of color photography at a time when color was widely viewed by art photographers as too decorative and too literal, aligned more closely with commercial photo and print media industries. Klute's images would go far to help change this perception. Not only would her photographs appear in a Kodak Data Book, small-format technical booklet for the amateur and professional photographer in 1951 (fig. 14), her work was put on the road in the form of various exhibitions and displays that visited trade shows, galleries and museums in the United States and around the world. Most importantly, influential museums included her work in exhibitions that sought to argue or promote the emerging position of color photography as an artistic medium. These included the Smithsonian, Royal Photographic Society of Great Britain, and a presentation of Klute's marine photographs, supported by Kodak, entitled *The Color of Water* (1965), that was displayed in thirty galleries and museums across the United States.

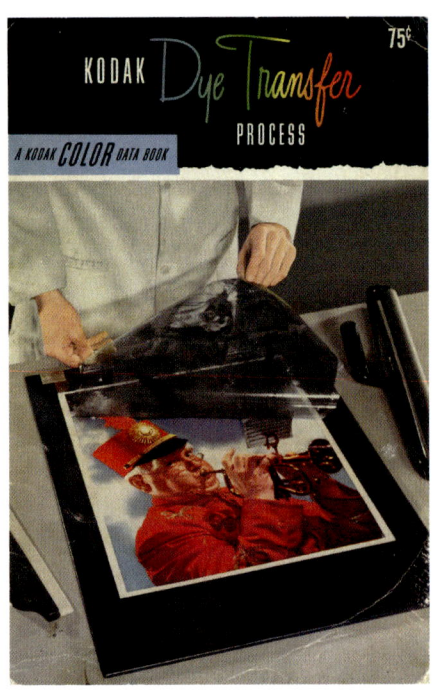

14. Kodak booklet, *Dye Transfer Process*, 1950. Used with permission from Eastman Kodak Company.

While Klute's nature photographs certainly caught the eye of the professional photographer and the public, so did her experimental work known as *Derivations*. Widely appreciated today in current literature defining the critical reception of color photography from its origins in the nineteenth century to our current digital age, *Derivations* were produced concurrent with Klute's woodland pictures. These images were the result of a working partnership between Klute and Dorothea Petersen, an engineer in the Visual Research Studio's labs in 1949. Writing in the preface of *Woodland Portraits*, Ralph Evans framed the experimental distinctiveness of the *Derivations*:

> [Klute] is as well or better known as the discoverer, with her technical associate Mrs. Petersen, of the processes now called "Derivations from Color Photographs." In these processes photographic color prints are produced in which the realism of color photography is almost wholly removed. They are abstractions in which the subject matter is clearly recognizable and not distorted, yet wholly unreal.[12]

The inventive process behind the experimental appearance of the *Derivations* first appeared in a Kodak Data Book in 1951 (fig. 15), in which the material and technique were described and illustrated with Klute's work. In its final appearance, the Derivation process presented the look of a color lithograph, diminishing visual contrast for a brightness and clarity of design, replete with color variations and patterns. As lead scientist of the Visual Research Studio's lab, Evans recalled the origination of the process in a chapter entitled Control in Printing for *Eye, Film, and Camera in Color Photography*:

> In the fall of 1949, a photographer [Klute] and an engineer [Petersen] working in the writer's (Evans) laboratory were led to combine two known techniques to study the result from an artistic point of view.... The photographer had reasoned that one of the difficulties with color photography, when an attempt was made to use it creatively, was the

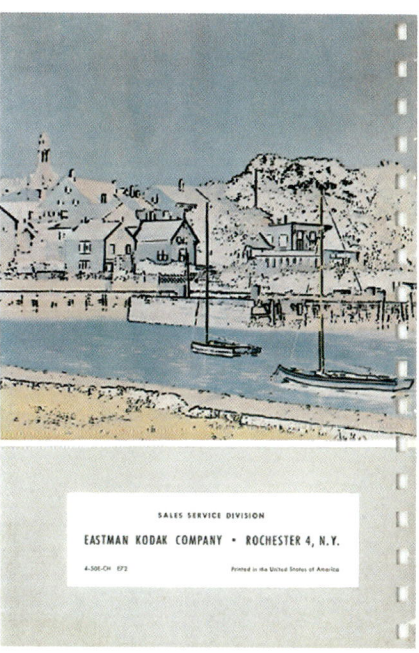

15. *Derivation*, from Kodak booklet *Derivations*, 1951. Used with permission from Eastman Kodak Company.

insistence of the objects in the picture and had made good progress in decreasing this insistence by "straight" photography.[13] (fig. 16)

Of the benefits of this new technique for color photography, Evans wrote:

> The basic importance behind this work lies not in the specific techniques nor in the individual pictures that can be made. It lies in the release of the color photographer from the necessity of realistic treatment whenever such release is called for by his subject. It also, for the first time, places the photographer in the role of a designer of patterns direct from nature without intervening hand work.[14]

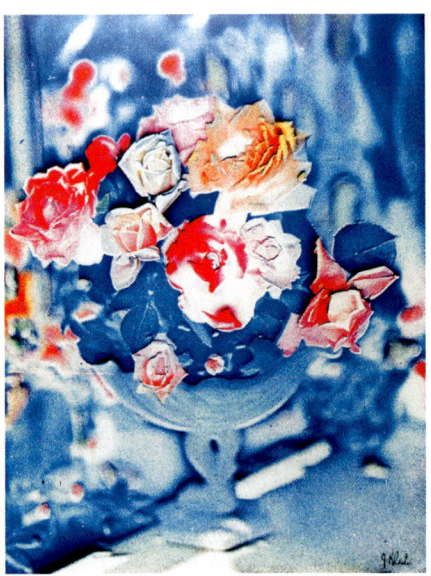

16. *Derivation*, 1951, RIT Archive Collections

For Evans, Klute's abstract *Derivations* along with her realistic *Woodland Portraits* served as illustrative bookends that supported his lifelong investigation in the ways photographers either offset or made use of 'accurate' color photographs for their 'particular purposes'. Evans' and Klute's relationship was a rare manager-and-employee symbiosis. Their interactions in the laboratory, in the pages of books and articles, monograph, and exhibited displays demonstrate the great advantages both realized from working together.

Klute's *Derivations* realized immediate admiration. Among her admirers was Ansel Adams, who during one of his visits to Kodak asked Klute and her team to use the Derivation process on some of his color plant images. Edward Steichen, photographer and then curator of the influential photography department at the Museum of Modern Art in New York City, surveyed the current status of color photography in the 1950 exhibition *All Color Photographs*. The exhibition featured 342 photographs and 70 photographers, and examined as Steichen commented for the exhibition's press release: "…the status of color photography as a creative medium. Is it a new medium for the artist or is it a means of supplementing or elaborating the recognized attainments of black and white photography?"[15] Along with documentary photography and descriptive, straightforward color photographs, the exhibition also highlighted abstract, experimental color work. In this latter section, Klute's *Derivations* were presented as were Adams', both produced by Klute and her team at Kodak. Concurrent with the run of the *All Color Photographs* exhibition, influential curator and photographic historian Beaumont Newhall at George Eastman House in Rochester, NY, introduced a touring exhibition of Klute's *Derivations* that visited more than twenty venues in the United States, England, Switzerland, and France. Beyond the rarefied walls of the museum and gallery, the *Derivations* received popular attention in photography magazines and journals, including *Popular Photography*, the London *Picture Post*, and *Image*, the journal of the George Eastman House, to name but a few. At a moment in photographic history when the question of color photography as an art form was hotly debated in photo-specialized and popular press, Klute's *Derivations* and its semi-descriptive, semi-abstract appearance pointed to the potential for creative photographers to expand the evolving experimental language of color photography.

FOCUS ON COLOR

The 1940s and 1950s were heady years for Klute. In the decade that followed, she sought to expand her audience through exhibition and publication. During the 1960s, her work was widely circulated by Kodak in touring exhibitions, such as the 1964 *Focus on Color*, and appeared in countless company publications, including annual reports, emphasizing the advancement and application of color photography. More exhibitions included the 1969 traveling exhibition *Discovering Color in Nature*, organized by the Smithsonian, and a display at *Expo 1969* in New York City. Closer to home, her reputation grew. In 1967, she was selected as a Fellow of the Rochester Museum of Arts and Sciences (now known as the Rochester Museum and Science Center) and Rochester-based printing company Stecher-Traung-Schmidt used many of her *Woodland Portraits* images to illustrate its annual reports from the mid- to late 1960s. Yet even given all of this successful activity, the tides of color photography in the United States were shifting away from Klute and other art photographers, like Adams and Porter, and the primacy of the finely-honed natural detail and/ or landscape view. An idealized or pristine natural world, so long a part of the lexicon of American photography was steadily supplanted by new photographic preoccupations with the American altered landscape, marked by the growth of suburbia and environmental management, as well as the social landscape. So too, was the emphasis on the photographer's expert handling of camera, film, and print technology. The introduction of popular color products, including the Polaroid camera and its "instant" film, Kodak's Instamatic pocket cameras, and low-cost color processing available at the corner drugstore gave tremendous rise to a new color snapshot aesthetic, grounded in the fast-changing American vernacular scene.

As color photography and its technology was dramatically changing, so too was Klute's role at Eastman Kodak. Beginning in the late 1960s and continuing into the 1970s, her last full decade at Kodak — she retired in 1982 — Klute was supervisor of the newly named Photographic Technology Studio. In this role, she was responsible for all research photographers and technicians. As supervisor, she took the remarkable step of hiring women to fill the majority of Studio positions. As Klute explained to her biographer: "...it's good to help prove to the world that women truly do have brains."[16] She also described this period as a photographer as her "commercial mode."[17] Klute was assigned to new low-end, consumer Kodak color products, in particular the Kodak Instamatic cameras and film. She was rightly recognized and promoted by Kodak for many years for her artistic work using its professional products, and the company now marketed Klute's photographic acumen to a burgeoning amateur market for color photographs, as seen in this commercial advertisement from 1973 (fig. 17). During this same period, Klute received what may be seen as one of the greatest acknowledgments of her work: her selection for the groundbreaking 1975 exhibition *Women in Photography, An Historical Survey*, in which Klute was recognized as an innovator of color photography. Five of her color photographs were include in the exhibition and all but two plant images were drawn from *Woodland Portraits*.

Of the thousands of women photographers considered for the *Women in Photography* exhibition, guest curators Margery Mann and Anne Noggle

**These pictures were taken
by a lady with a
Kodak pocket Instamatic® 60 camera.**

**There was nothing special
about the camera,
but the lady is a bit special.**

Her name is Jeannette Klute, and her job
with us is to show what can be accomplished
with our products, given experience.
Ms. Klute joined us quite a few years ago
in a routine job, as boring as most people's
jobs. Then a miracle transformed her: she
developed a personal interest in the products.

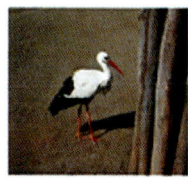

A visit to the San Diego Zoo

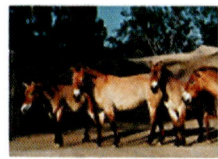

Equus przewalskii,
very rare species of wild horse

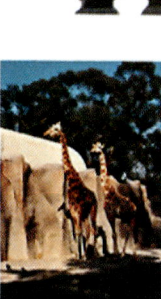

**A little frankness
because there is too much to lose
when people come to distrust advertising**

If everybody expected photographic results like
Klute's every time a shutter clicked, we'd be in
trouble. Buying a set of oil paints and an artist's
easel never made anybody an artist. Buying a camera, film, and processing service is a considerably
better deal. You have a high probability of getting
pictures. If you want them to be more than an aid
in remembering where, what, and whom you saw on
a certain pleasant occasion, you must take a few
pains, learn a few things there isn't room for in the
instruction booklet, and play the percentages. Even
Klute takes a lot of pictures that nobody else ever
sees.

For those who do want to learn, Kodak publishes
a great deal of how-to-do-it literature. For a guide to
that literature with order blank, send a self-addressed
envelope prominently marked "A3-75" to Kodak,
Dept. 55W, Rochester, N.Y. 14650. (Some of the
books it describes might be appreciated as gifts by
the photographically ambitious.)

Literature helps and experience helps more, including experience in finding a processing service
whose standards satisfy you. Fortunately there is a
wide choice, depending on how much you value ex-
cellence.

17. Kodak advertisement featuring Klute's photographs, taken with an Instamatic camera,
1973. Used with permission from Eastman Kodak Company.

selected only fifty to tell the story of women's achievements in photography:

> The idea in basic concept was to bring together works by those
> women photographers who have, throughout the history of the
> medium's functioning life, made distinguished contributions to
> the broadening pattern of our culture.[18]

The introduction of this exhibition directly corresponded to the concerns
of the feminist movement of the 1960s and 1970s. Its purpose was to recast
the history of photography from the perspective of women photographers,
who had long been excluded from much of photographic literature. In
the exhibition catalogue, Noggle spoke to the personal and professional
convictions embraced by the exhibited women photographers:

> There is a corollary between their assertiveness and their accom-
> plishments. One thought is consistently expressed by those who
> have achieved recognition and success: an unsolicited, emphatic
> denial of discrimination against them in their work, or of being
> hampered in any way.[19]

In her intertwining roles as a research photographer and as an art photographer, Klute confirmed time and again her pioneering spirit as she forged
professional applications for new color photographic technology with
artistic implications. She broke through the line between gender roles in
the workplace that acutely defined women's work from men's work. And
in her turn as manager, she prioritized hiring women for positions previ-
ously held by men. In these unprecedented ways, Klute was a trailblazer,
breaking new ground in the emerging field of modern color photography
and in the workplace.

THE LATER YEARS 1982–2009
Upon her retirement from Kodak in 1982, Klute gave up photography
as her artistic medium of choice, since she no longer had access to her
professional lab. Instead she began to paint in earnest, starting what she

called a "second career."[20] She also indulged lifelong interests. She further developed the property at her home in South Bristol, NY (fig. 18), increasing it from an initial 5 acres to 170 acres. Enlarging and reseeding the pond just beyond her back door was another constant endeavor. The natural views and floral details the pond provided informed her now painterly art. Klute cultivated a love for music, in particular playing the recorder. She had traveled to France to study the recorder and had once hosted a baroque music workshop on her property. With South Bristol neighbors, she formed a recorder quintet.

But in her retirement years, Klute did not leave photography behind entirely. She established Woodland Studio, a retail venue, in her home. Papers and correspondence held in the RIT Archives indicate that she spent much time selling her photographs and other photographers' images she had acquired, such as those of Ansel Adams, to museums, galleries, and collectors. She pursued display opportunities for her photography and paintings in locations in and around her home in the Finger Lakes, including the Naples Open Studio Trail, of which Klute was an originator along with fellow regional artists. On a larger scale, her work was shown in important exhibitions that appraised color landscape photography of the 1940s and 1950s. Amon Carter Museum's senior curator of photographs, John Rohrbach, visited Klute in preparation for his 2002 exhibition *Woodland Portraits: Photographs by Elliot Porter and Jeannette Klute*. In 2013, four years after Klute's death, Rohrbach included a *Derivation* in his significant 2013 exhibition publication entitled *Color, American Photography Transformed*. As these recent exhibitions convey, Klute continues to be remembered as a vital and integral figure in the history of photography for her contributions to the artistic and technical realm of modern color photography.

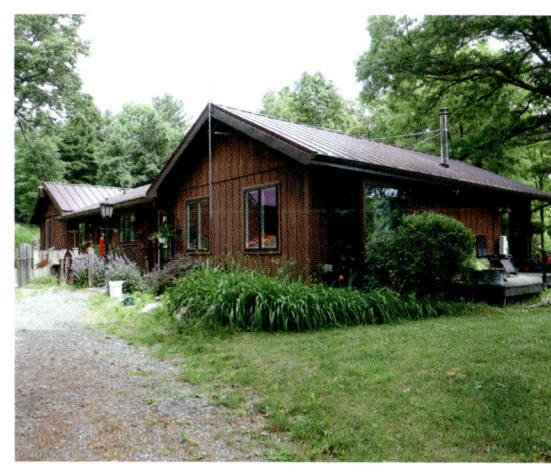

18. Jeannette Klute's home in South Bristol, NY. Since the photographer's death in 2009, her home has been renovated with new rooms added. Photo courtesy of Therese Mulligan.

Therese Mulligan, Ph.D.
Director, William Harris Gallery
Rochester Institute of Technology

NOTES

1   Kat Nichols, *Jeannette Klute, Photographer* (Rochester: Jeannette Klute Collection, 2008), unpaginated. This biography appeared on the Naples Open Trail Studio website during Klute's membership in the organization. Following Klute's death, the biography was deleted from the website and not archived. A copy of the biography from the website is housed in the RIT Archives.

2   In 1943, Klute acquired a Bachelor of Science degree in General Studies from the University of Rochester. She studied art history, among other subjects.

3   Herbert T. Kalmus. "*An Introduction of Color*, by Ralph M. Evans," *Journal of SMPTE*, February (1948): 236-237.

4   Ralph M. Evans. *Eye, Film, and Camera in Color Photography*. (New York: John Wiley & Sons, 1959), v.

5   Ibid., vi.

6   Jeannette Klute. *Woodland Portraits*. (Boston: Little, Brown and Company, 1954), unpaginated.

7   Ibid., Preface, unpaginated.

8   Ibid., Author's Note, unpaginated.

9   Ibid., Plate 1, unpaginated.

10 Evans, *Eye, Film, and Camera in Color Photography*, 13.

11 Ansel Adams, letter to Milton Rusk, publisher, Little, Brown and Company, September 25, 1954.

12 Evans, Preface in *Woodland Portraits*, unpaginated.

13 Evans, *Eye, Film, and Camera in Color Photography*, 350.

14 Ibid., 250.

15 Edward Steichen, *All Color Photography* Exhibition Press Release, Museum of Modern Art, 1950, 2.

16 Barbara Erbland quoted by Mark Hare, Jeannette Klute's obituary, *Democrat & Chronicle*, September 20, 2009, 3B and 5B.

17 Nichols, *Jeannette Klute, Photographer*, 2008, unpaginated.

18 John Humphrey, Introduction to *Women in Photography, An Historical Survey*, (San Francisco: San Francisco Museum of Art, 1975), unpaginated.

19 Anne Noggle, Essay in *Women in Photography, An Historical Survey*, unpaginated.

20 Jeannette Klute, *The Story of My Life in Five Minutes*, undated and unpaginated. This short-form autobiography was presented by Klute to a class at RIT Athenaeum entitled "My Place in the Universe."

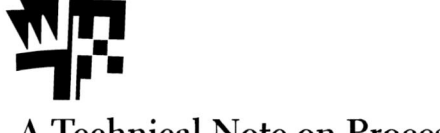

A Technical Note on Process

DYE TRANSFER PRINTING

A Dye Transfer print is a color print made of dyes transferred from three gelatin relief images, known as matrices, onto a sheet of paper coated with gelatin. The resulting prints have a fidelity and richness that photographers and viewers particularly value. There are several ways to derive the printing matrices: from a color transparency, color negatives, or from color separation negatives recorded in a special three-color camera. If starting with a color transparency, the original is projected through individual red, green and blue filters to divide the colors into three black and white separation negatives. Next, gelatin matrix film that can absorb the primary printing dyes (respectively, cyan, magenta and yellow) are exposed through the negatives. The matrices are then washed to remove the gelatin in the unexposed areas, creating a very thin relief in which the thickness varies with the density. Each matrix soaks up the dye in proportion to the thickness of the gelatin. In a process, much like that of offset magazine printing, the three matrices are then transferred in perfect registration to the paper's surface, where the gelatin absorbs the dye to create a full-color image.

DERIVATIONS

As a response to the realism of color photography, makers experimented with manipulating the process of color transfer to yield a more artistic product. The term *derivation*, in this case, denotes an image that has been produced by altering (or omitting) one or more aspects of the process. This could involve dyeing the matrices colors other than cyan, magenta,

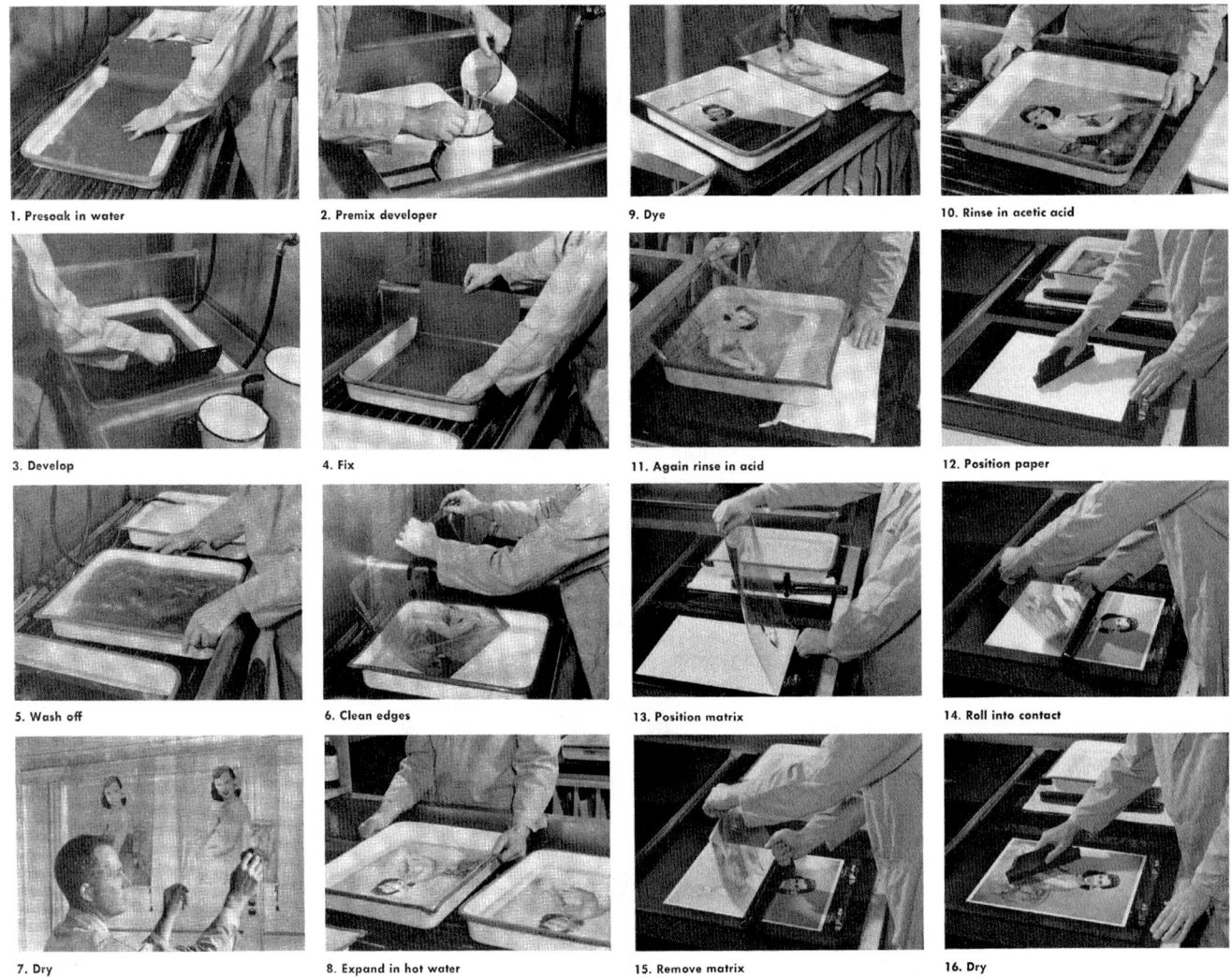

1. Presoak in water

2. Premix developer

9. Dye

10. Rinse in acetic acid

3. Develop

4. Fix

11. Again rinse in acid

12. Position paper

5. Wash off

6. Clean edges

13. Position matrix

14. Roll into contact

7. Dry

8. Expand in hot water

15. Remove matrix

16. Dry

Kodak Dye Transfer Process. A Kodak Color Data Book.
Rochester, NY, Eastman Kodak Company, pp. 4–5.

Jeannette Klute

and yellow, or by manipulation of contrast, or by a combination of color and density changes. One method involves creating a mask of the highlights of the image and likewise one of the overall visual density. When slightly offset from the original, the masks can produce a line contour of the image, creating a pen-and-ink effect. The image is now composed of a separate negative for visual density, the highlights, three color separations for the color, and a line contour. The possibilities are endless; the highlights can be represented as contour lines, the visual density omitted altogether, and matrices dyed. Recombined as a new Dye Transfer print, these manipulations of color and density range can result in a distortion of perceived depth in the image.

PRESERVATION

While dye-stability has been a longtime concern for the preservation of chromogenic prints and negatives, color separation negatives are an excellent, though expensive, means of preserving moving and still color images. Because the red, green, and blue negatives produced from an original color print are on black and white film stock, they do not risk dye-fading, and can be recombined to produce a faithful facsimile of the original color range.

Lauren Alberque
Project Archivist
RIT Archive Collections

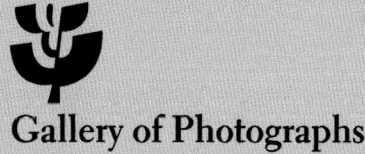

Gallery of Photographs

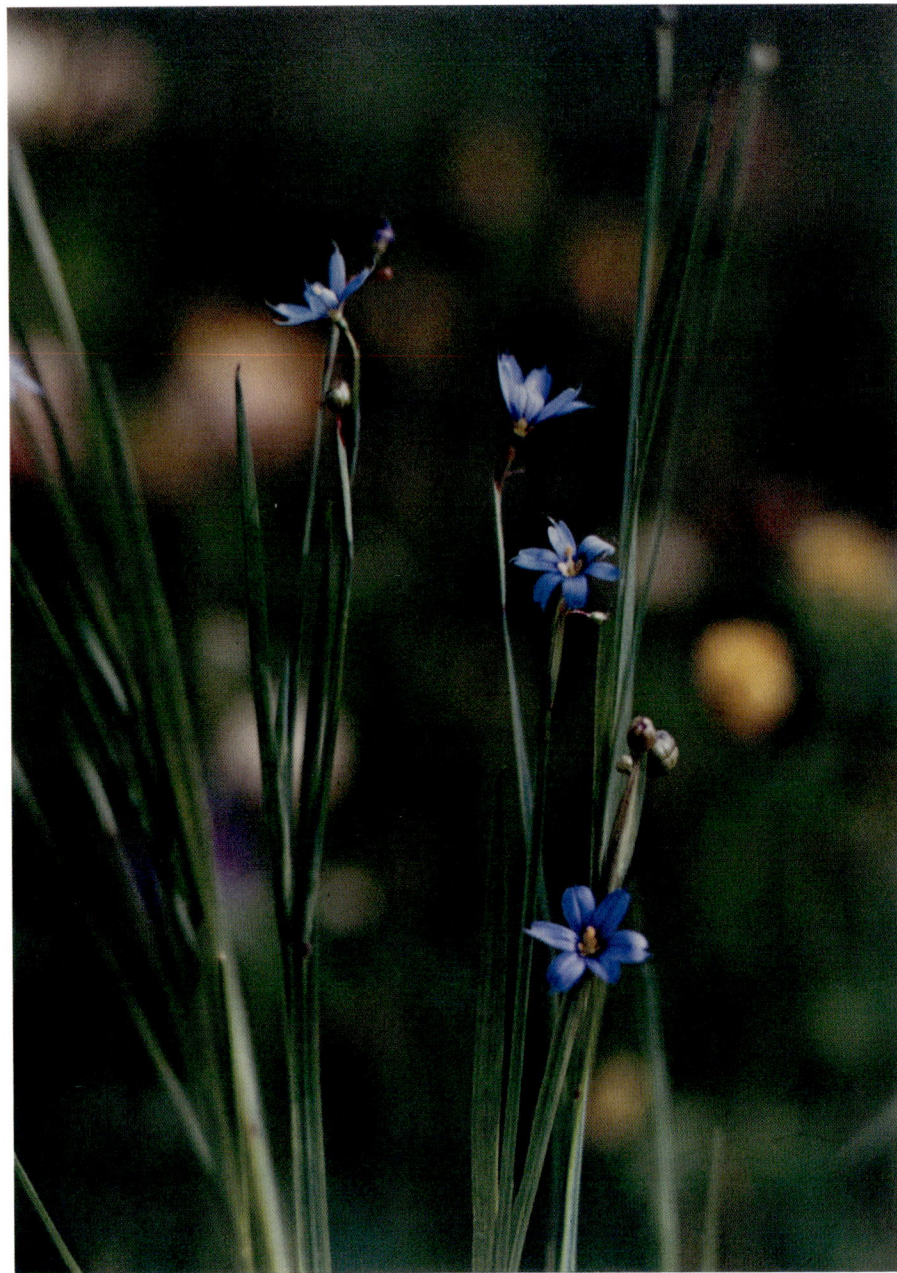

Blue Eyed Grass

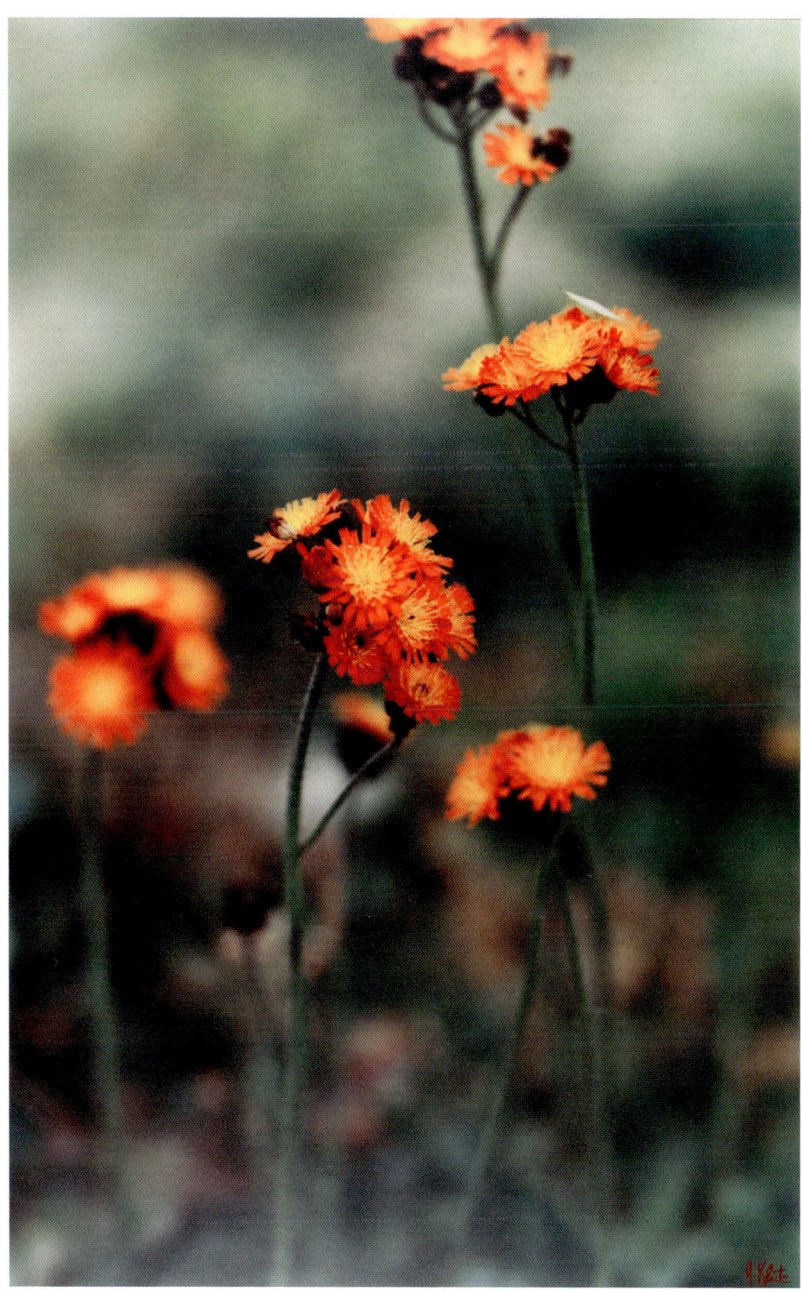

Hawkweed

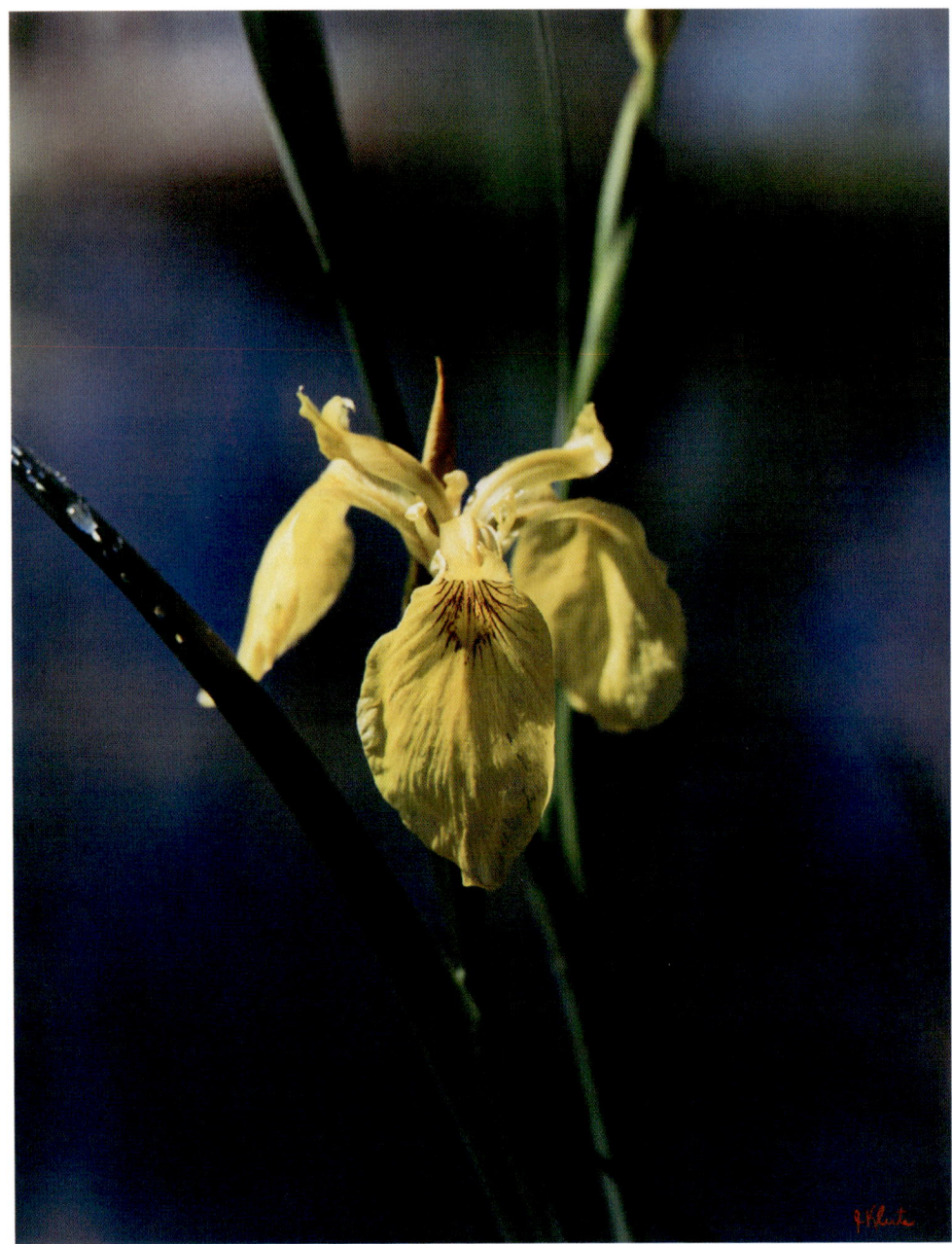

Yellow Iris

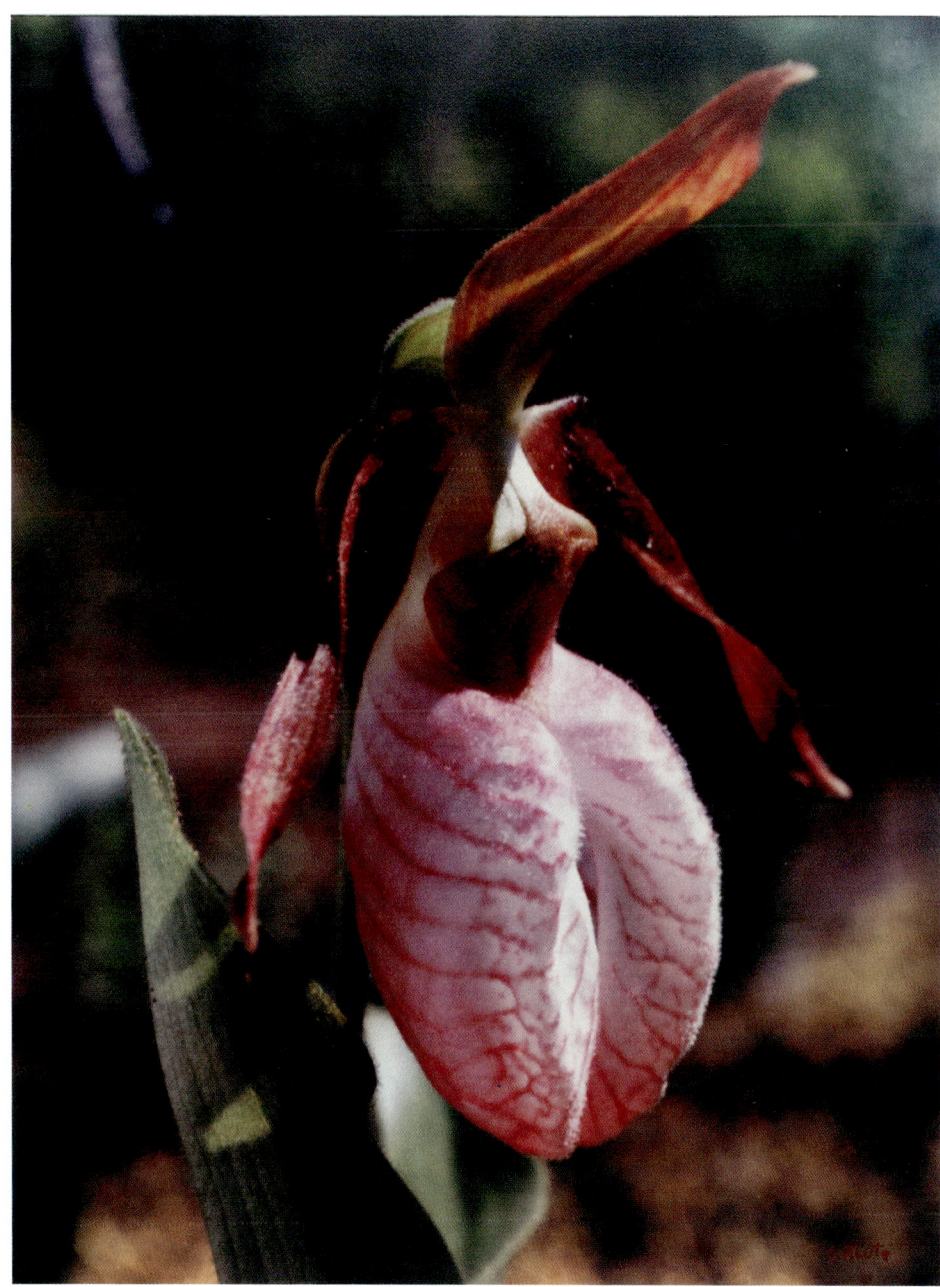

Stemless Lady's-slipper

29

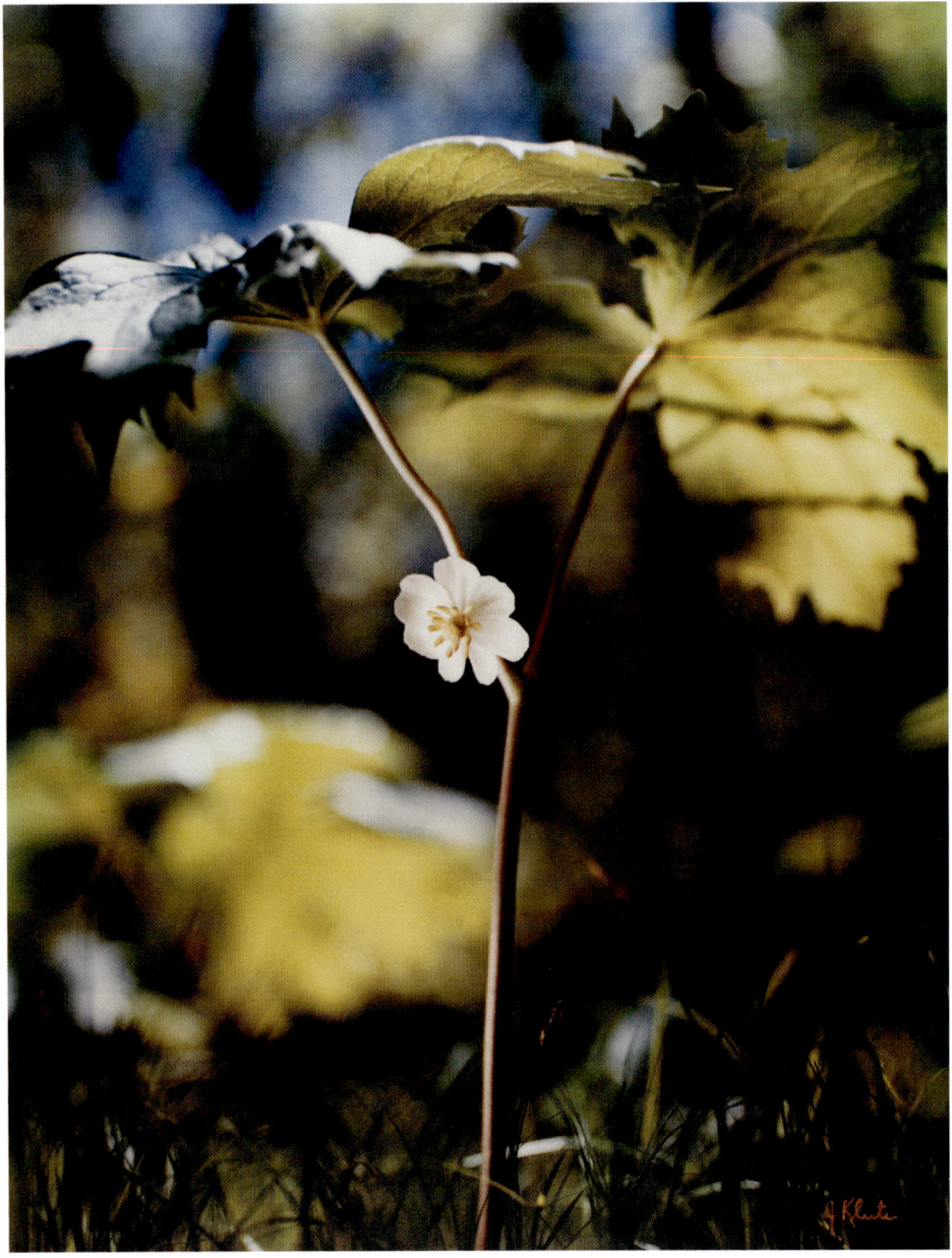

May Apple

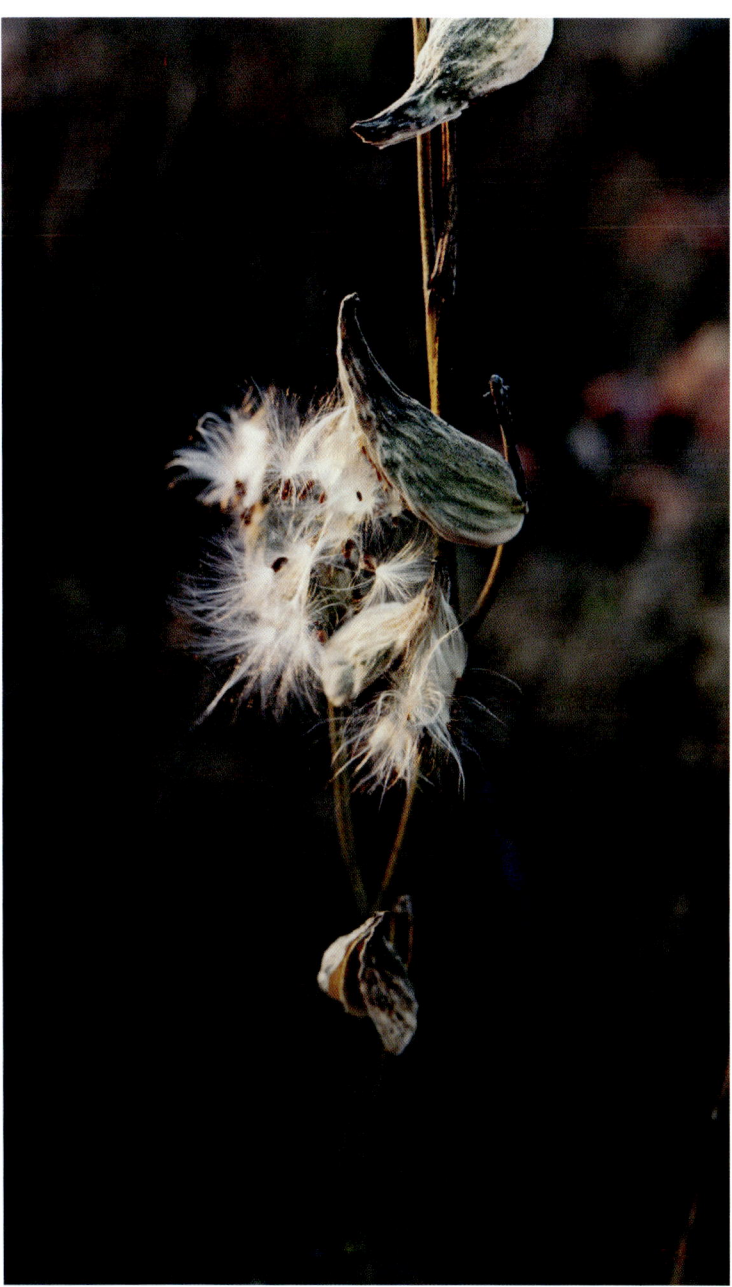

Milkweed

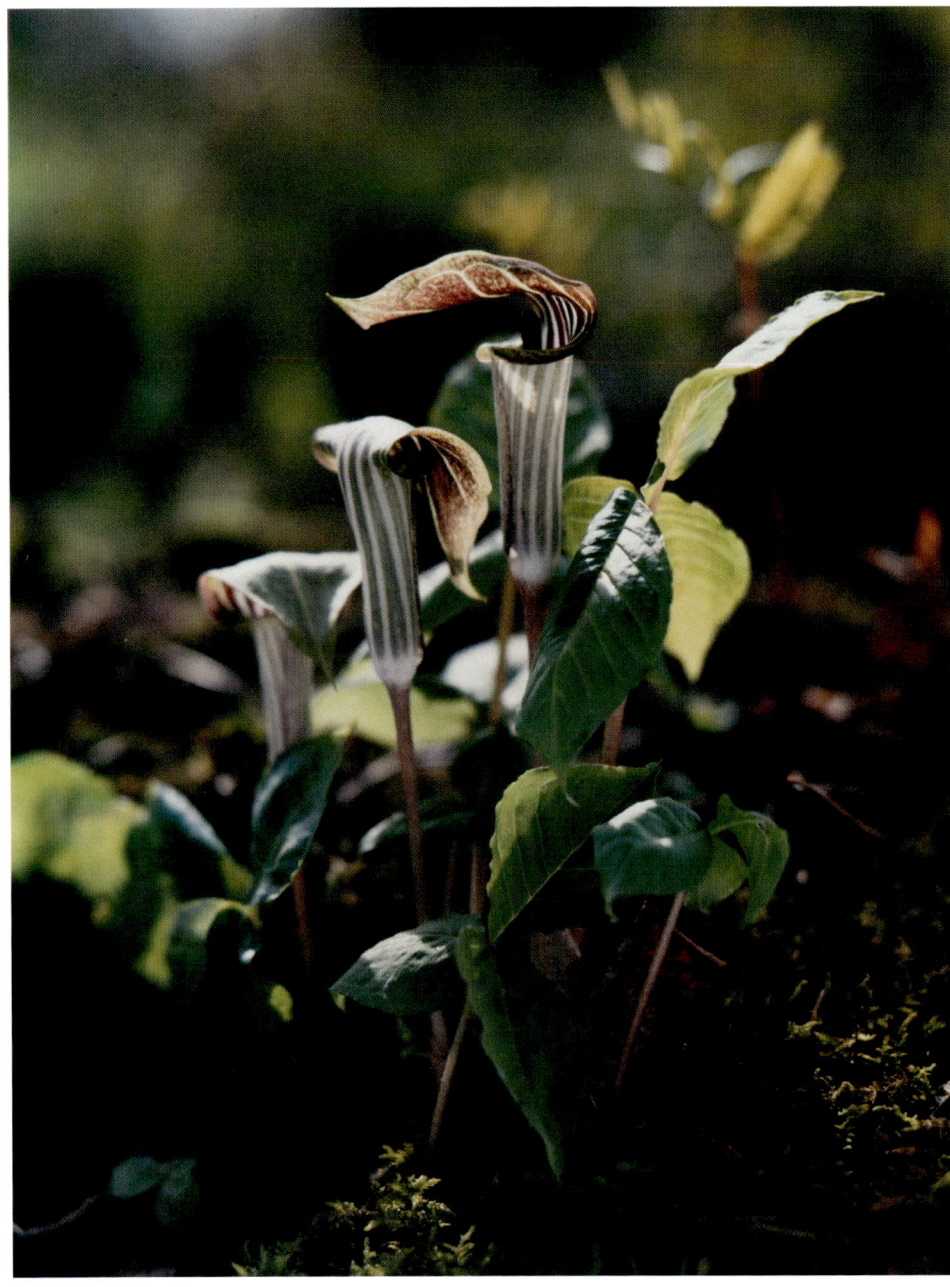

Jack in the Pulpit

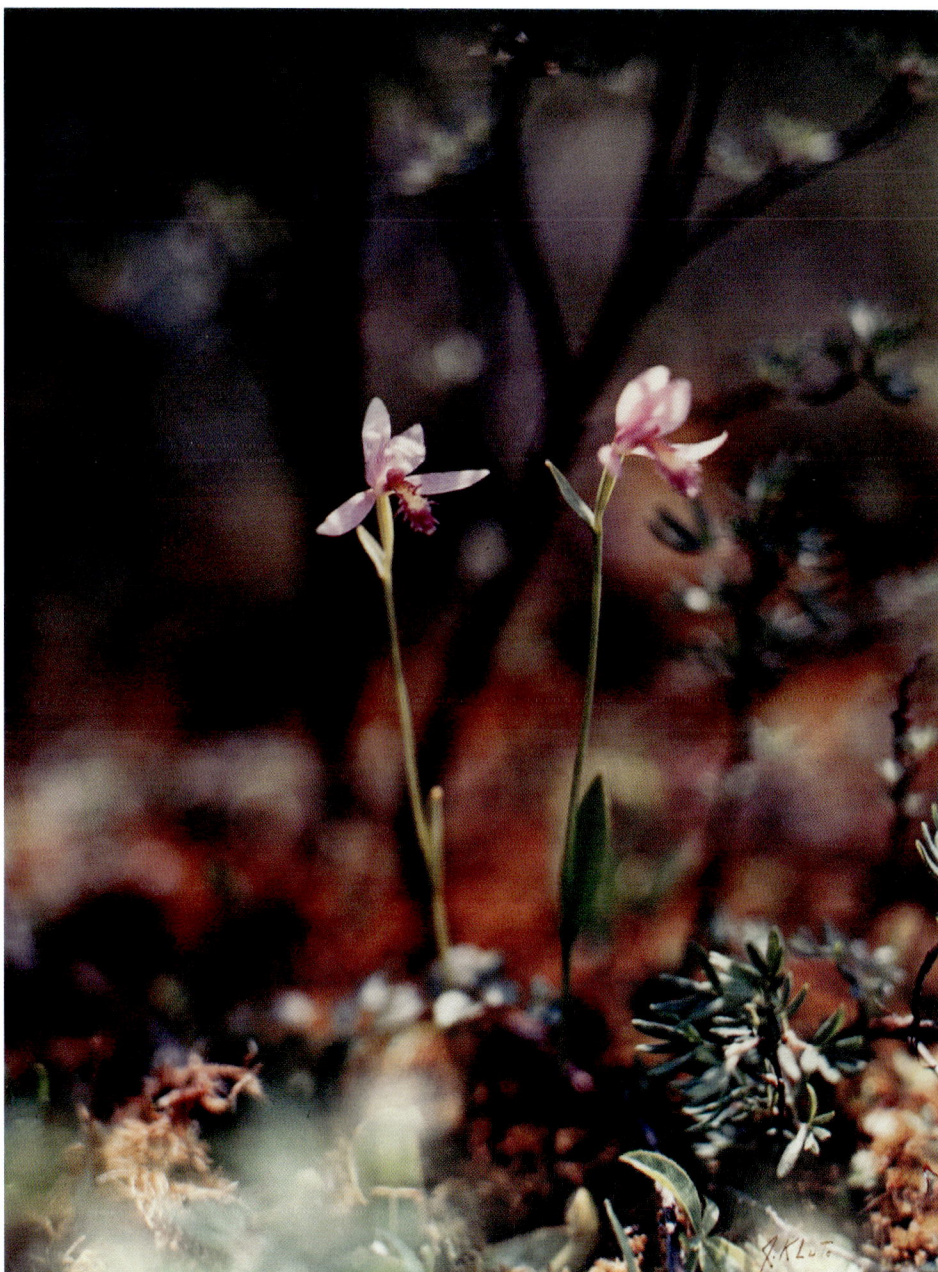

Pogonia

33

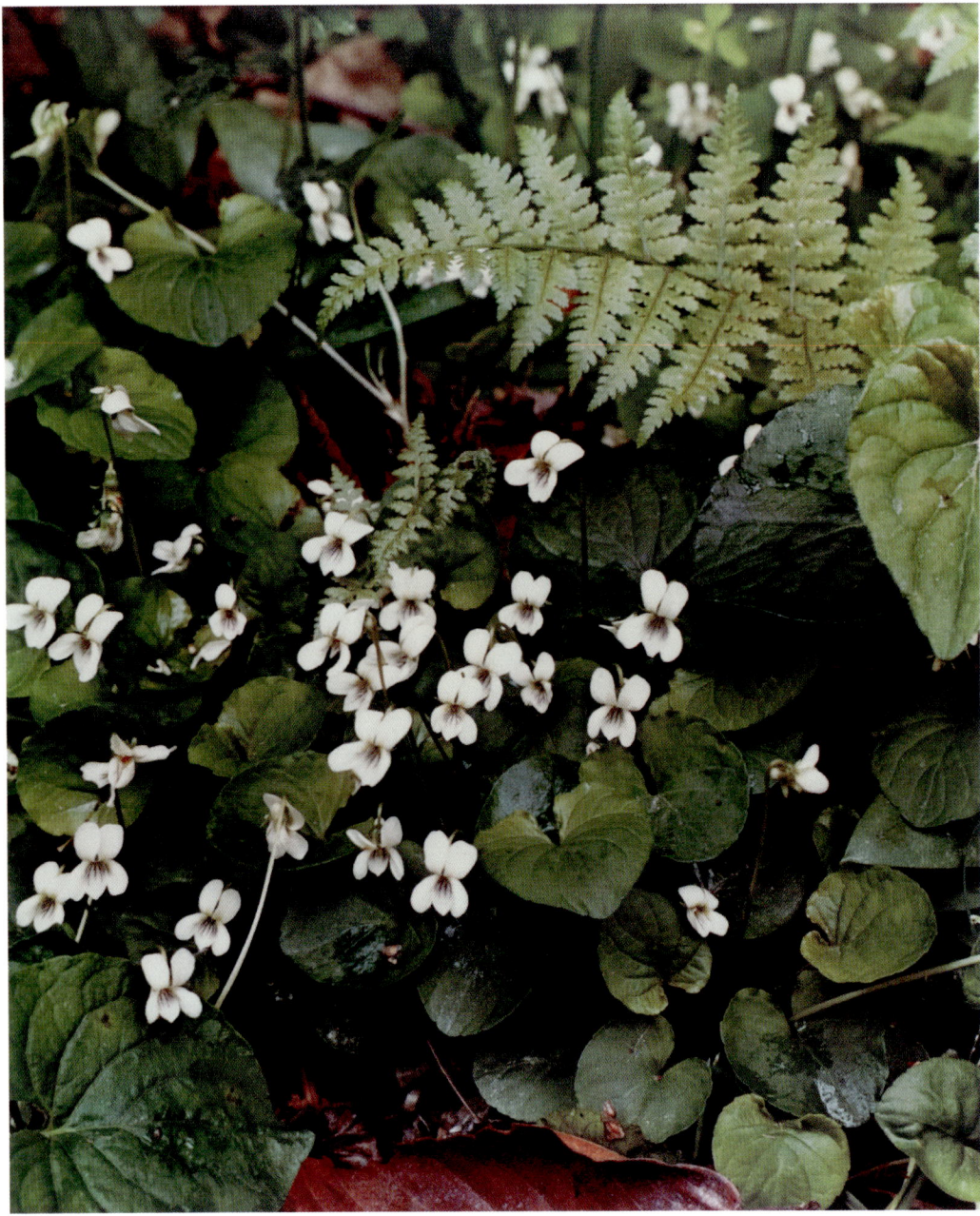

White Violet

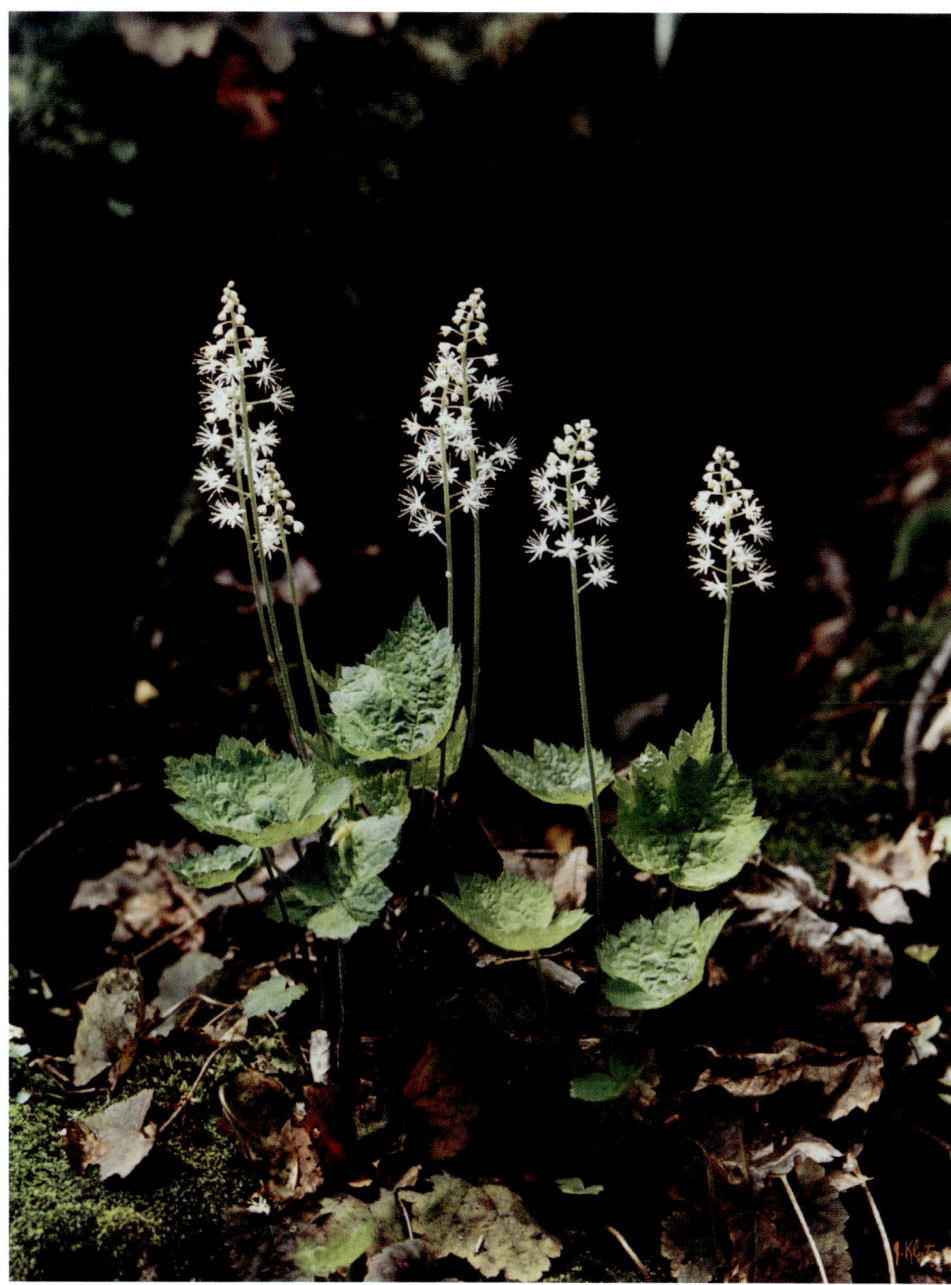

Foam Flower

35

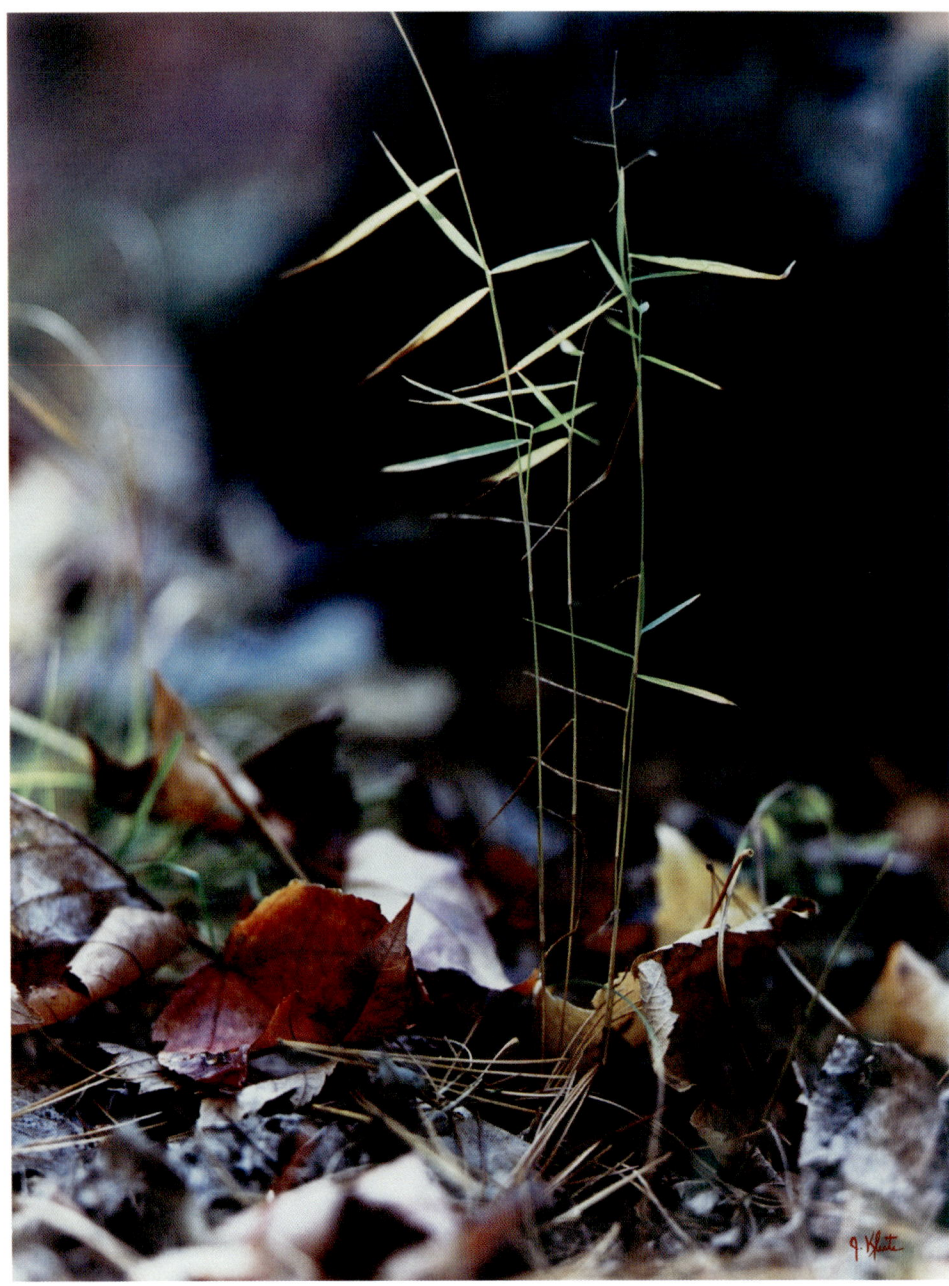

Grasses with Red Leaf

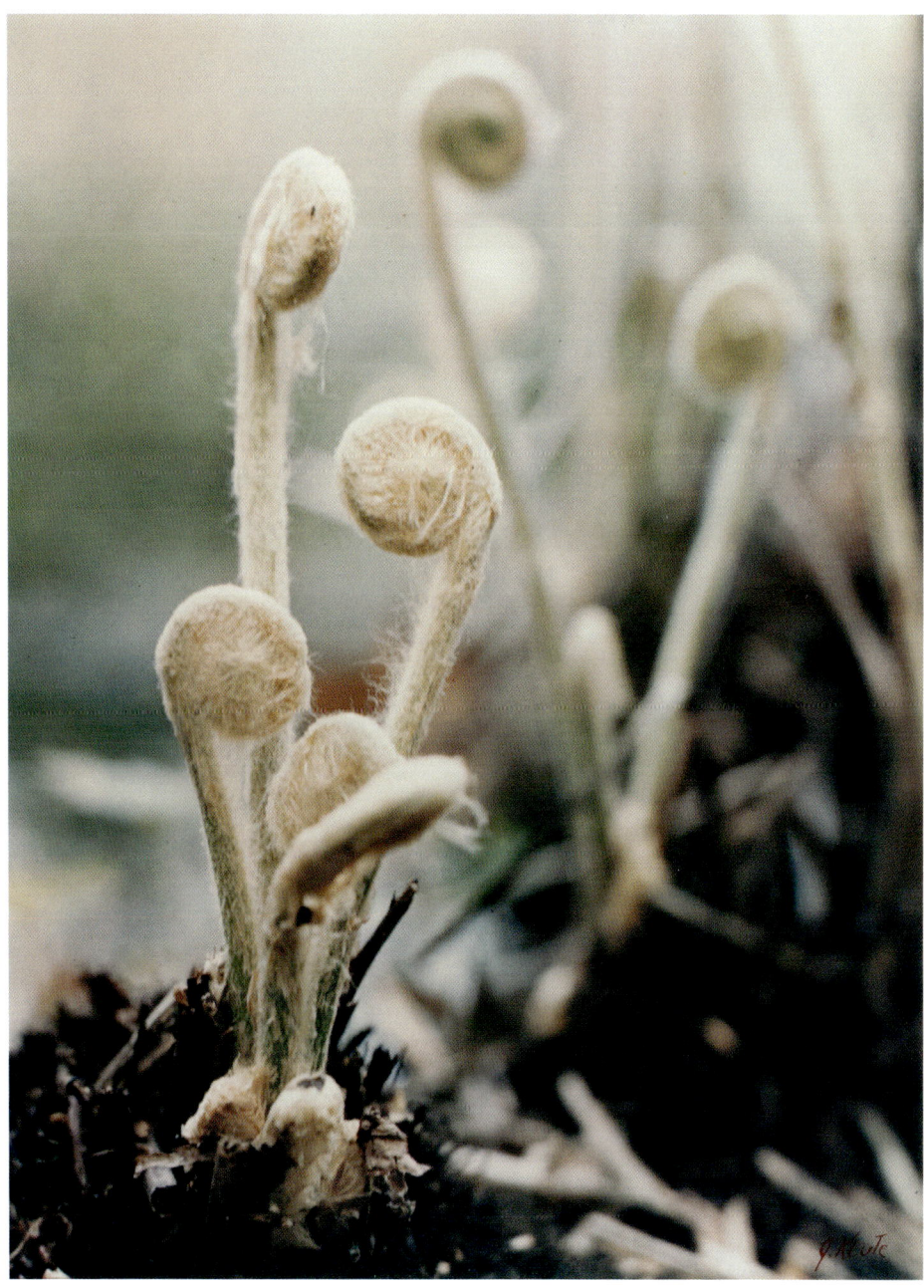

Cinnamon Fern

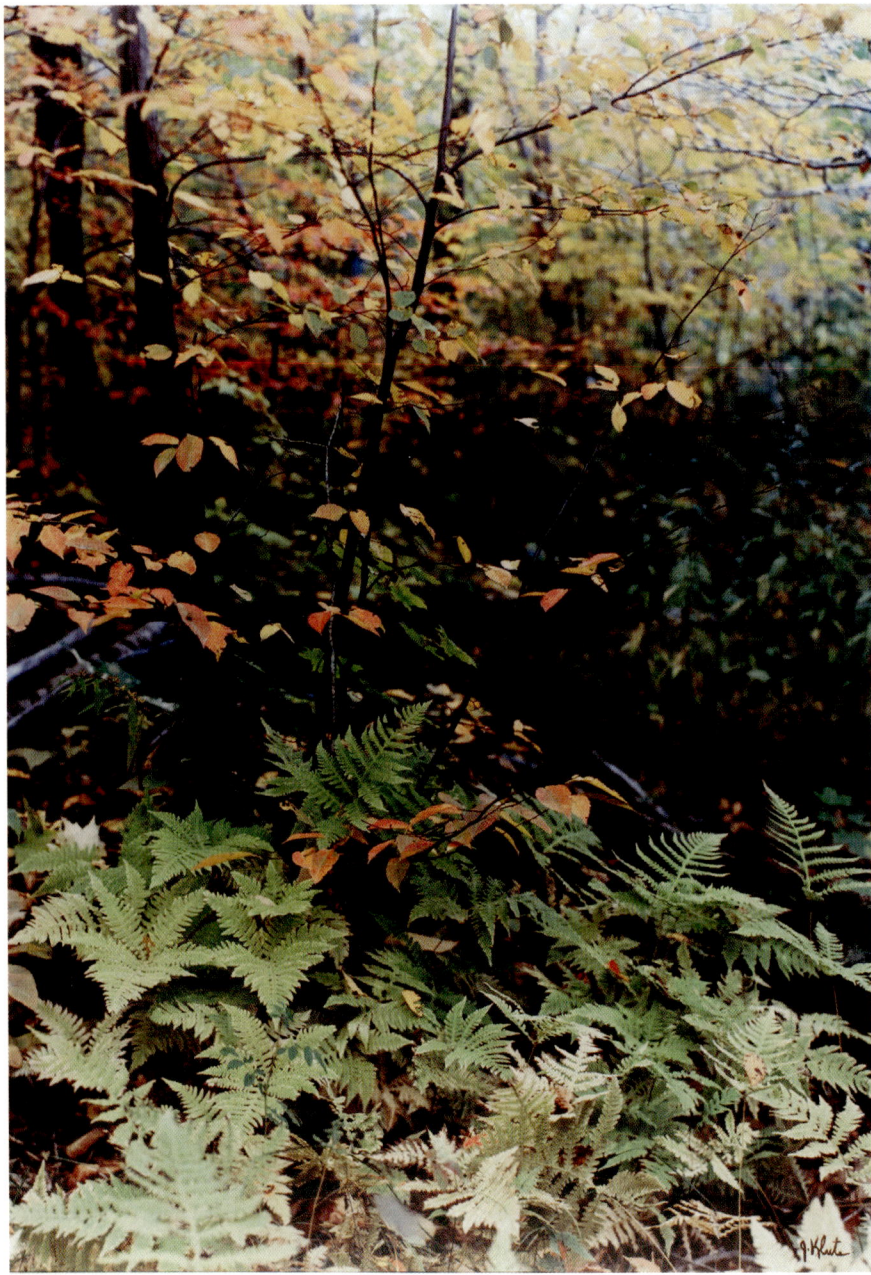

Beech Ferns in Woods

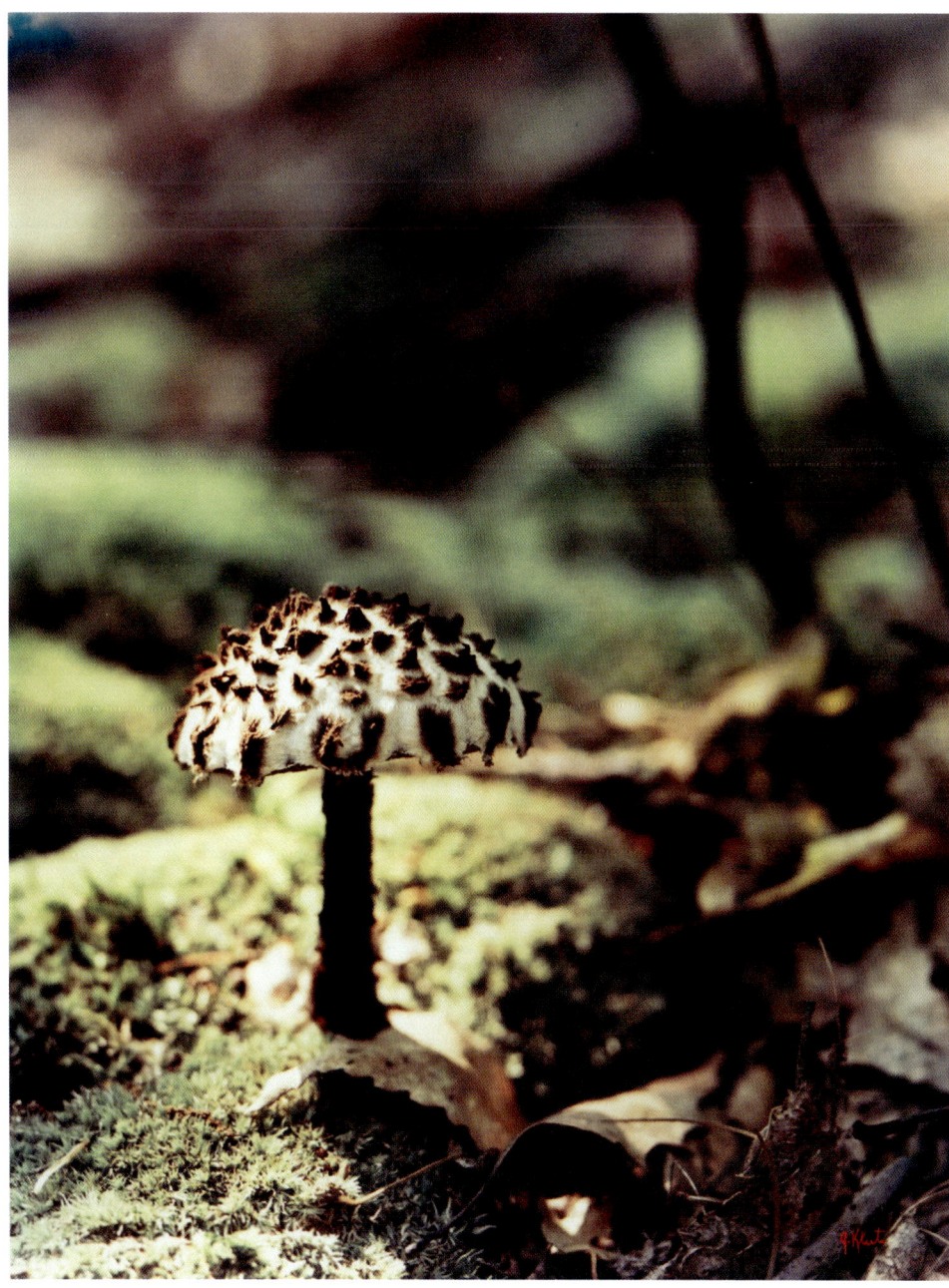

Pine Cone Mushroom

39

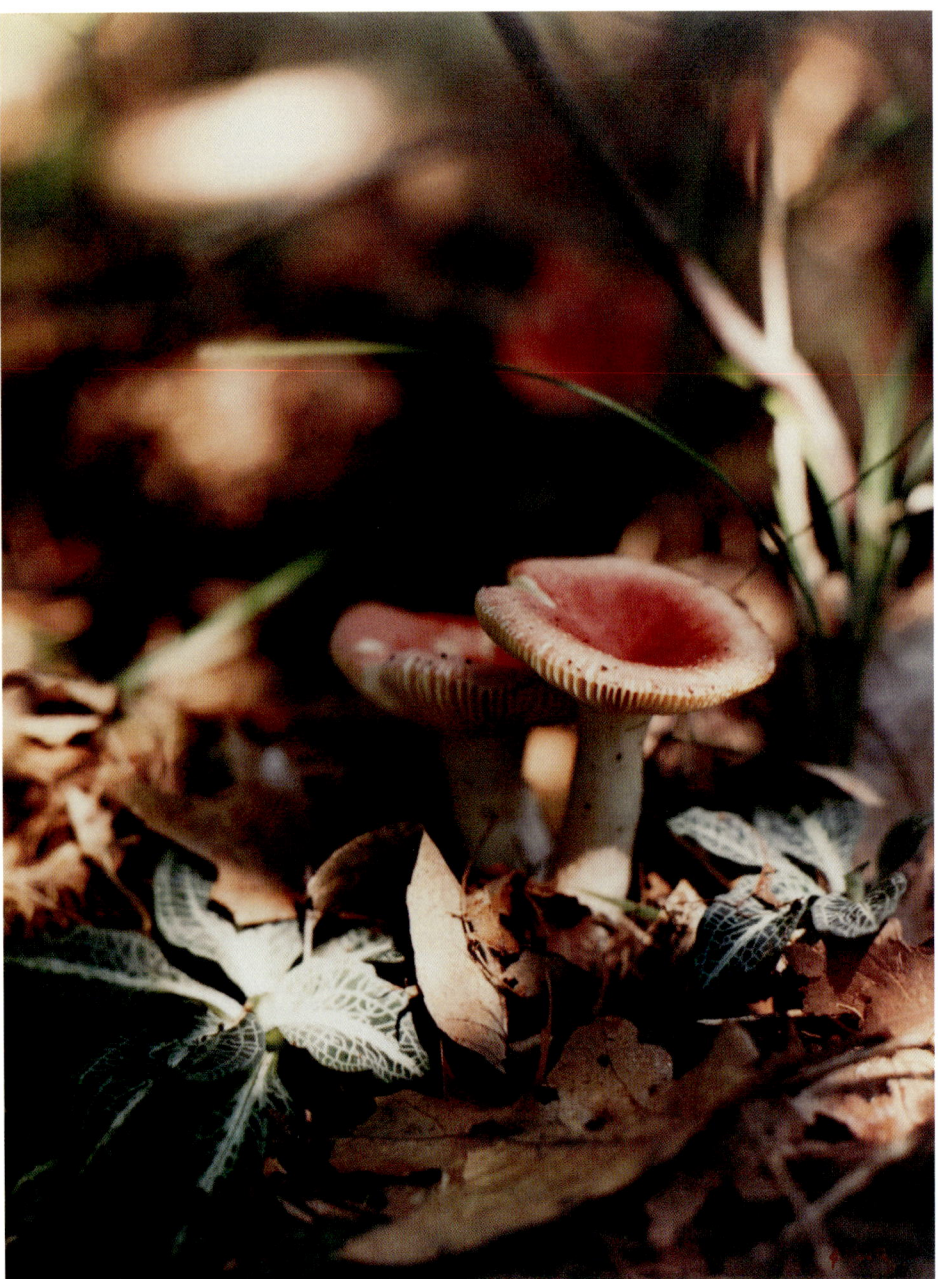

Mushrooms

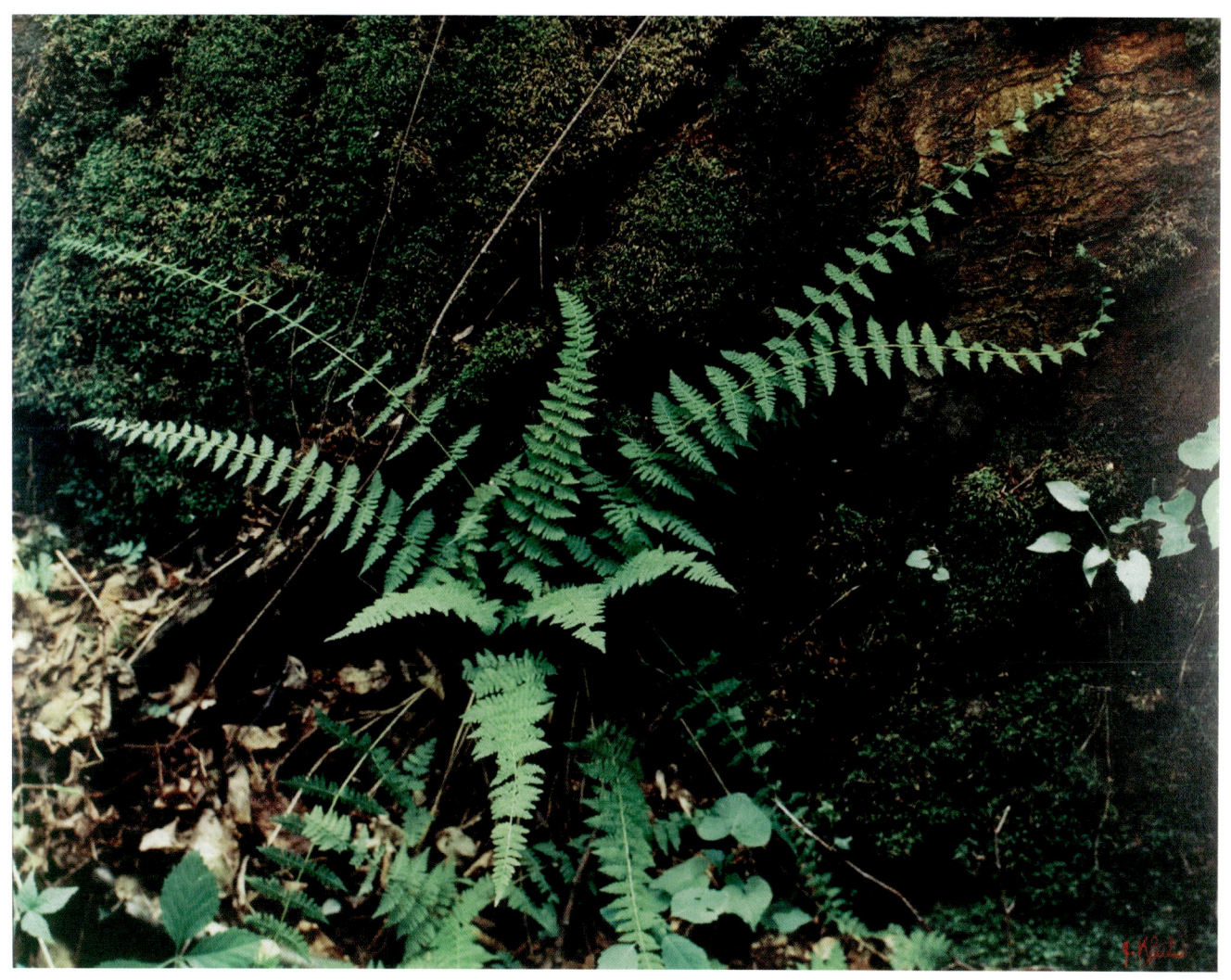

Fern on Moss

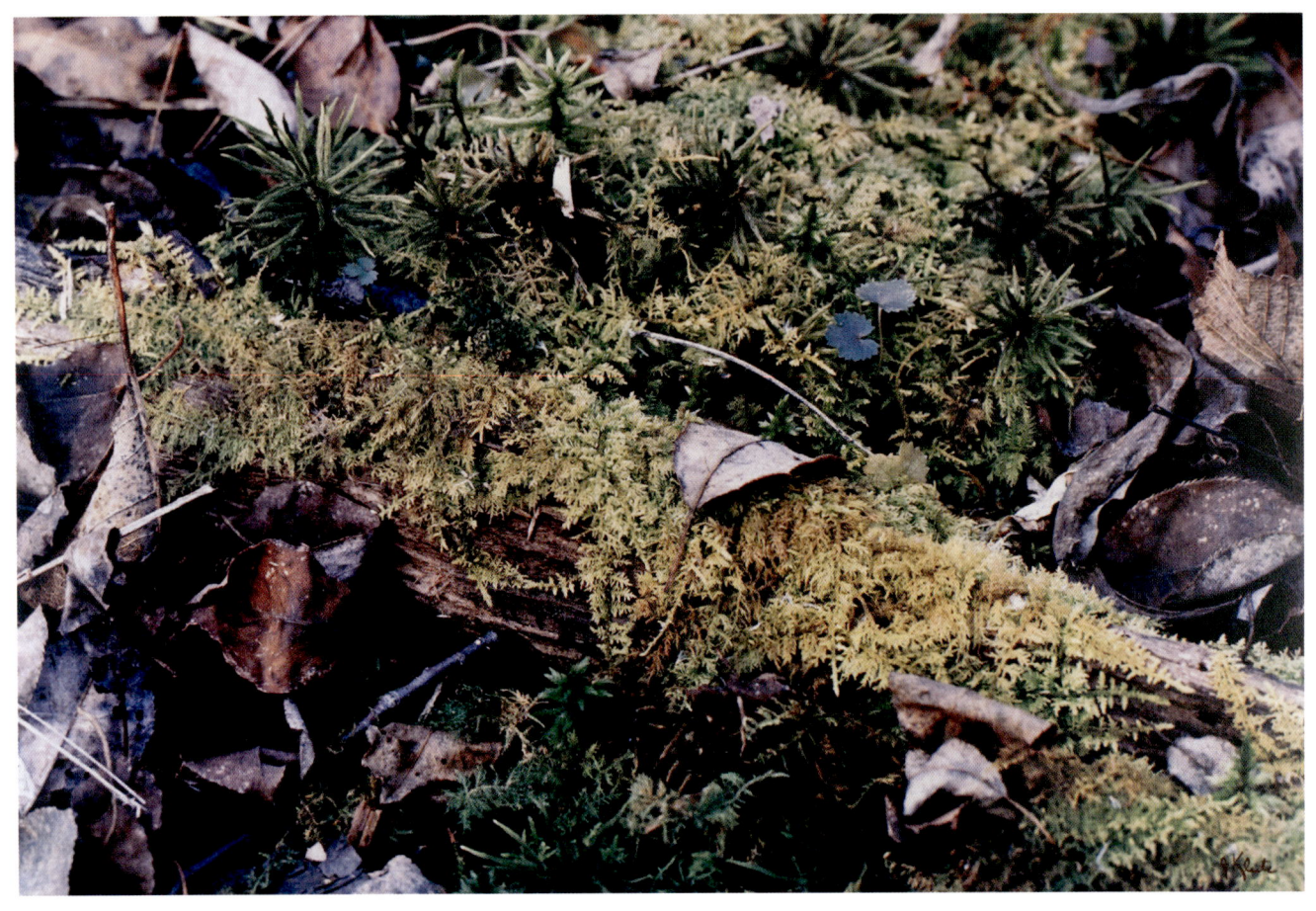

Moss on Log

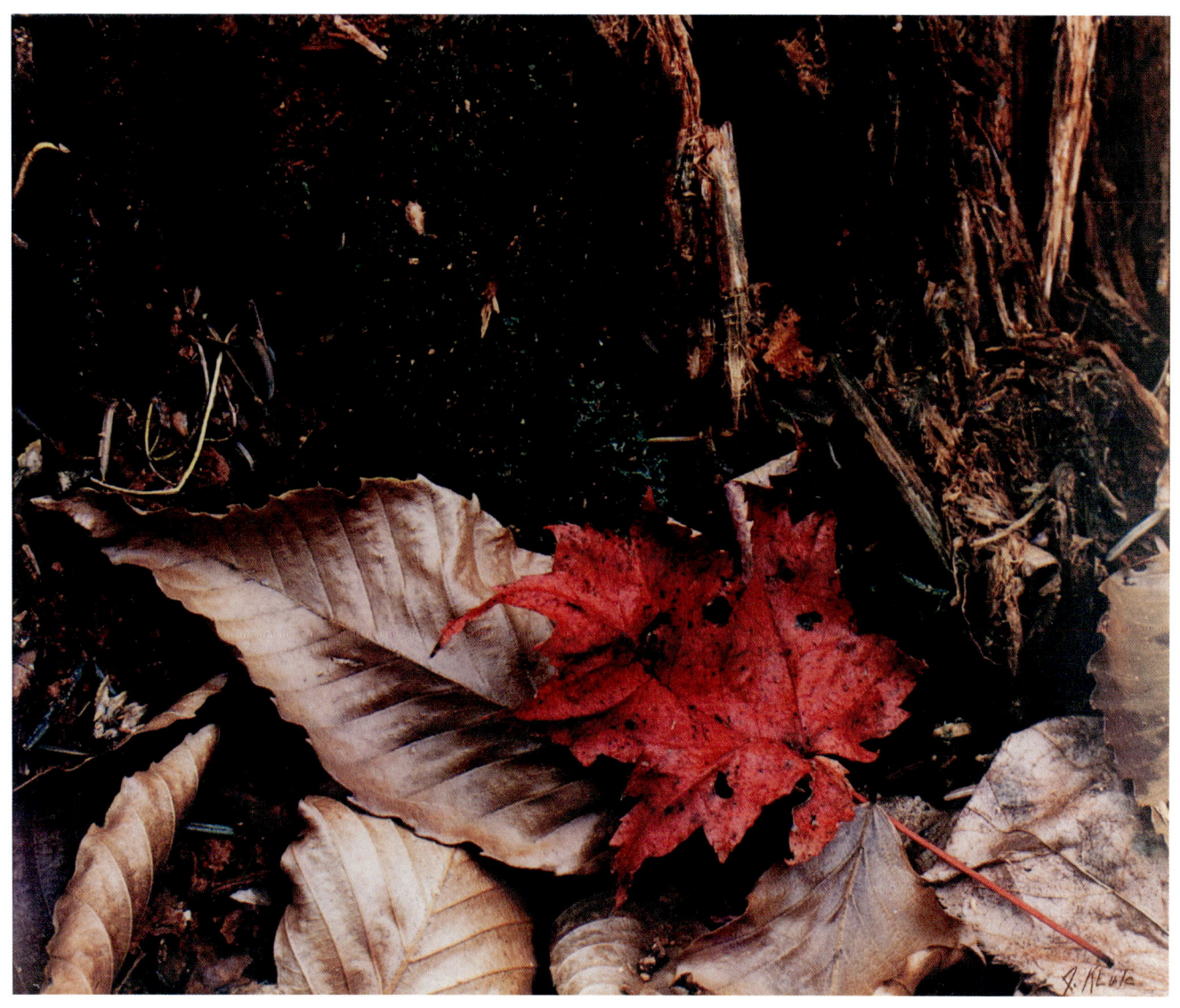

Beech and Maple

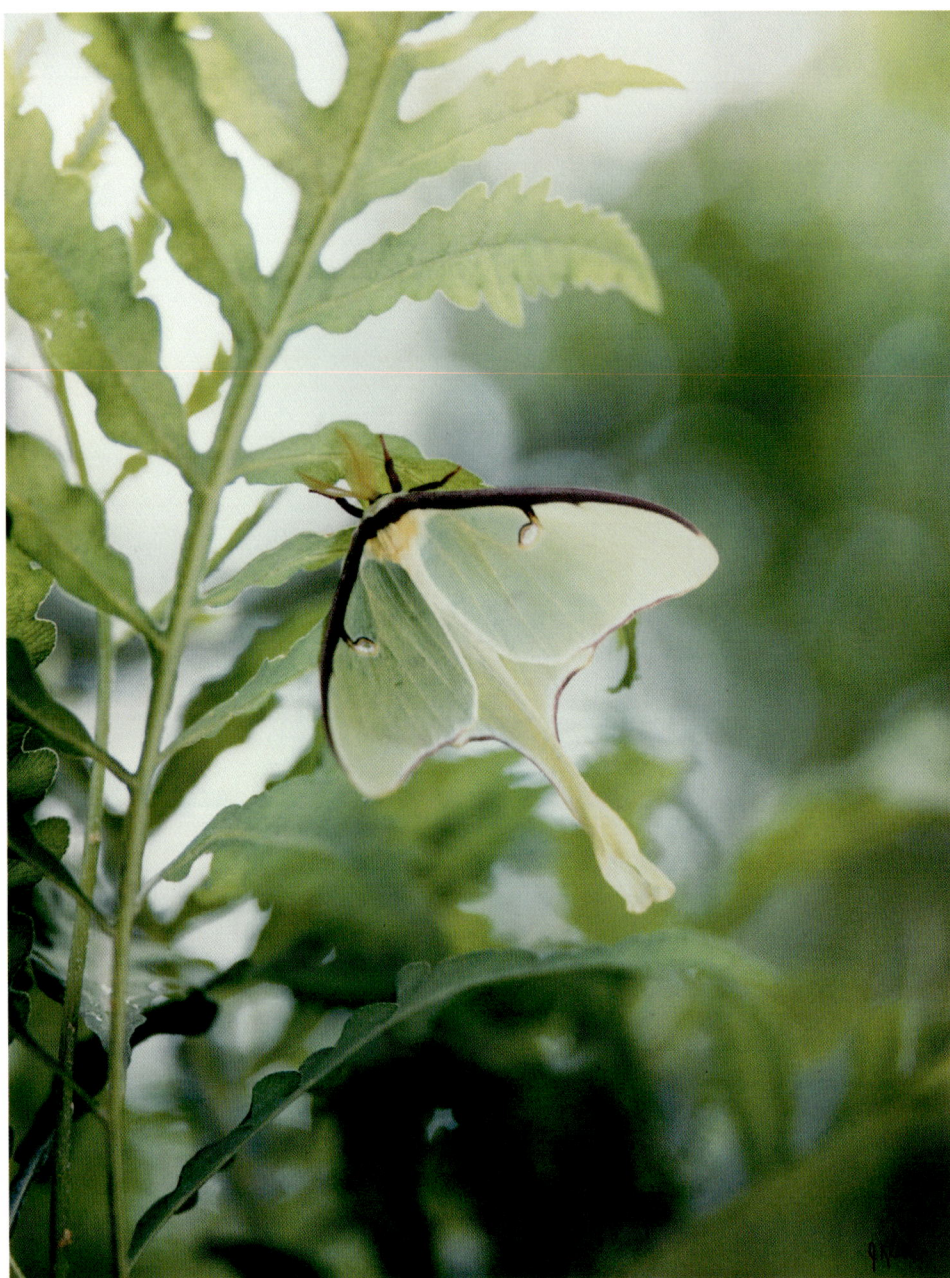

Luna Moth

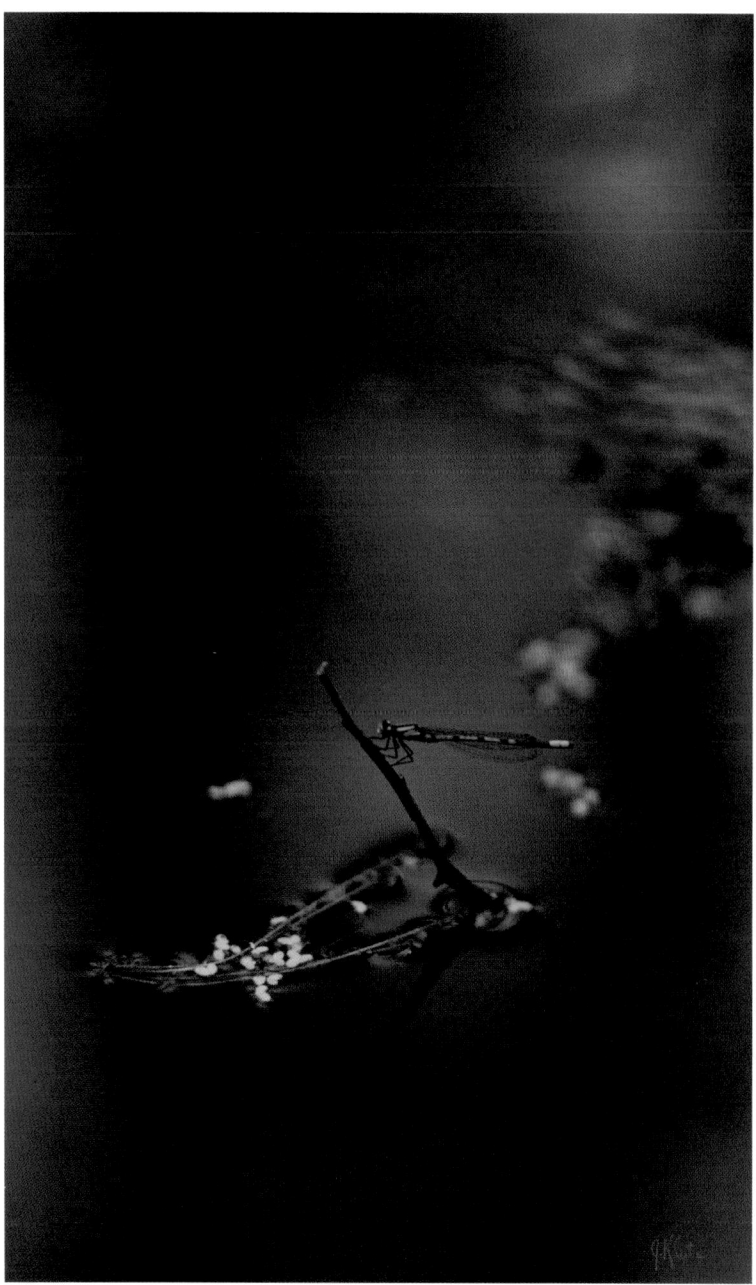

Blue Dragonfly

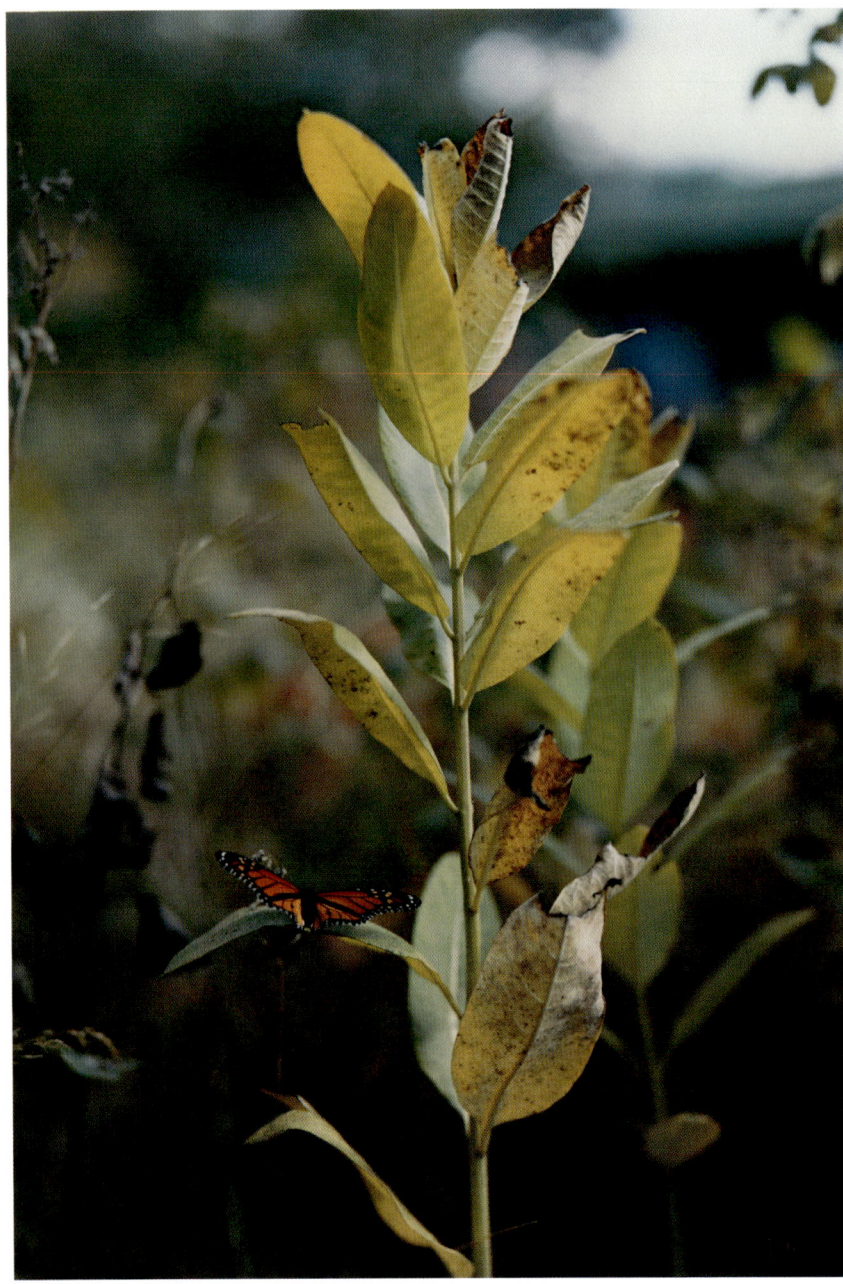

Milkweed with Butterfly

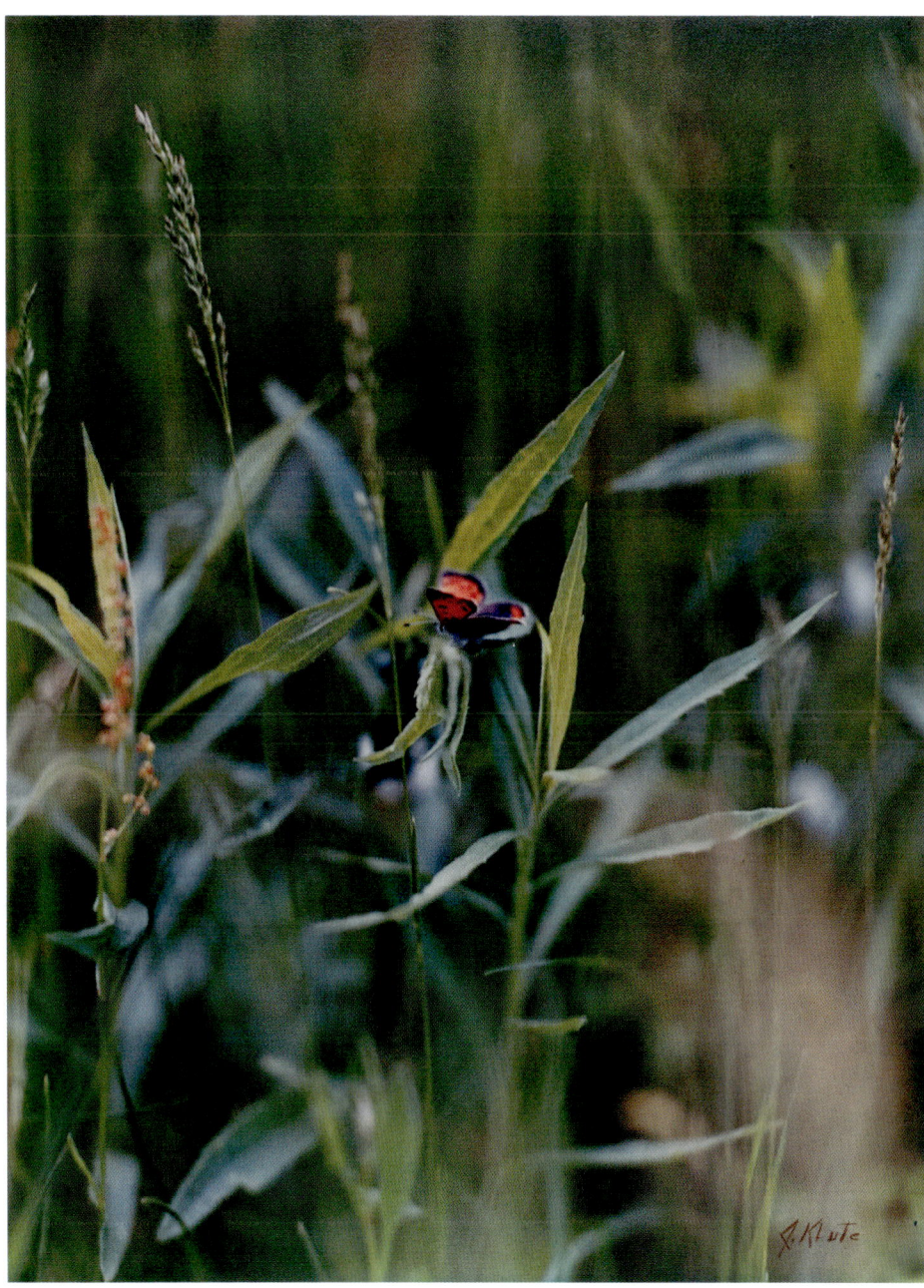

American Copper

47

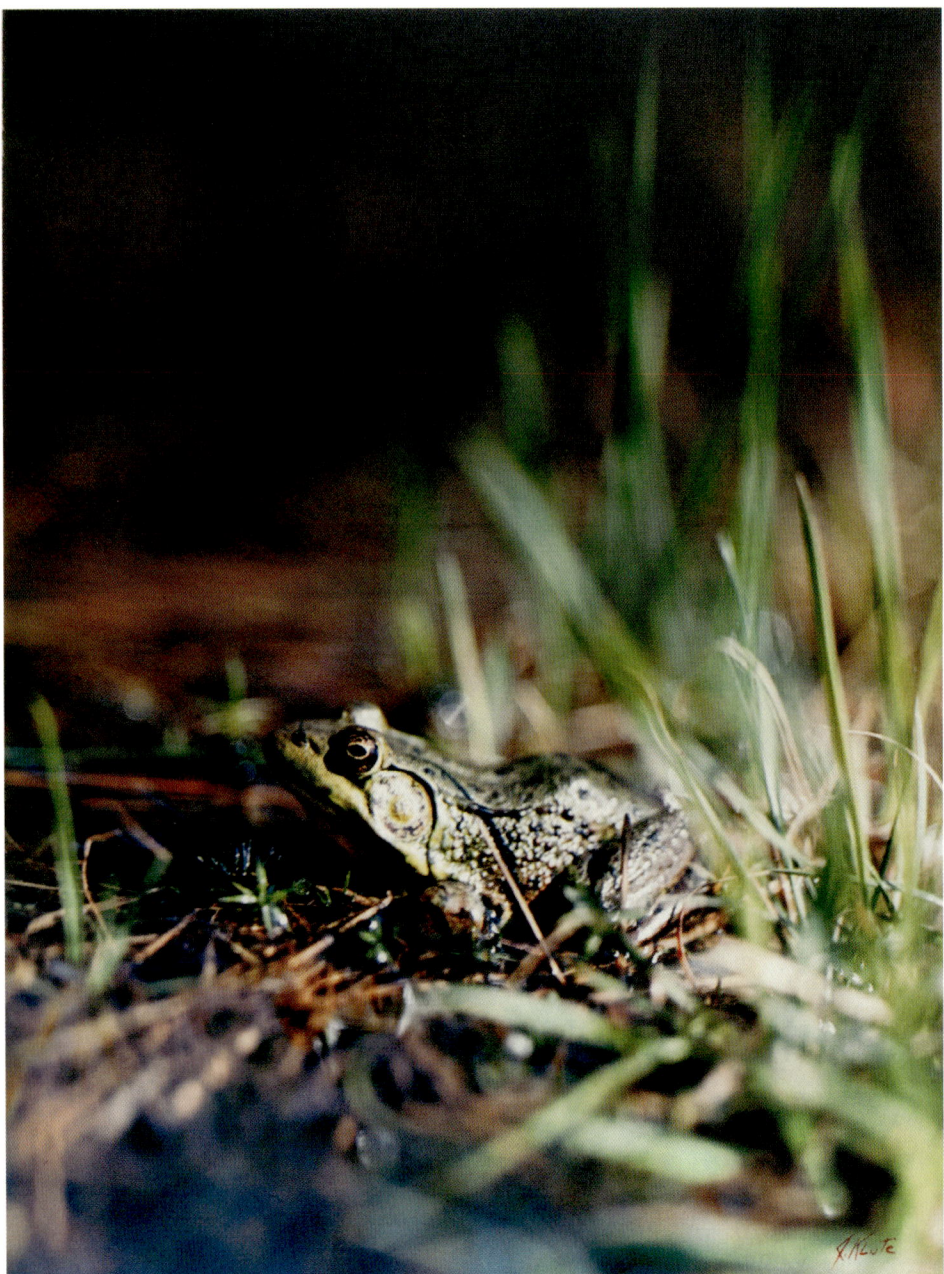

Green Frog

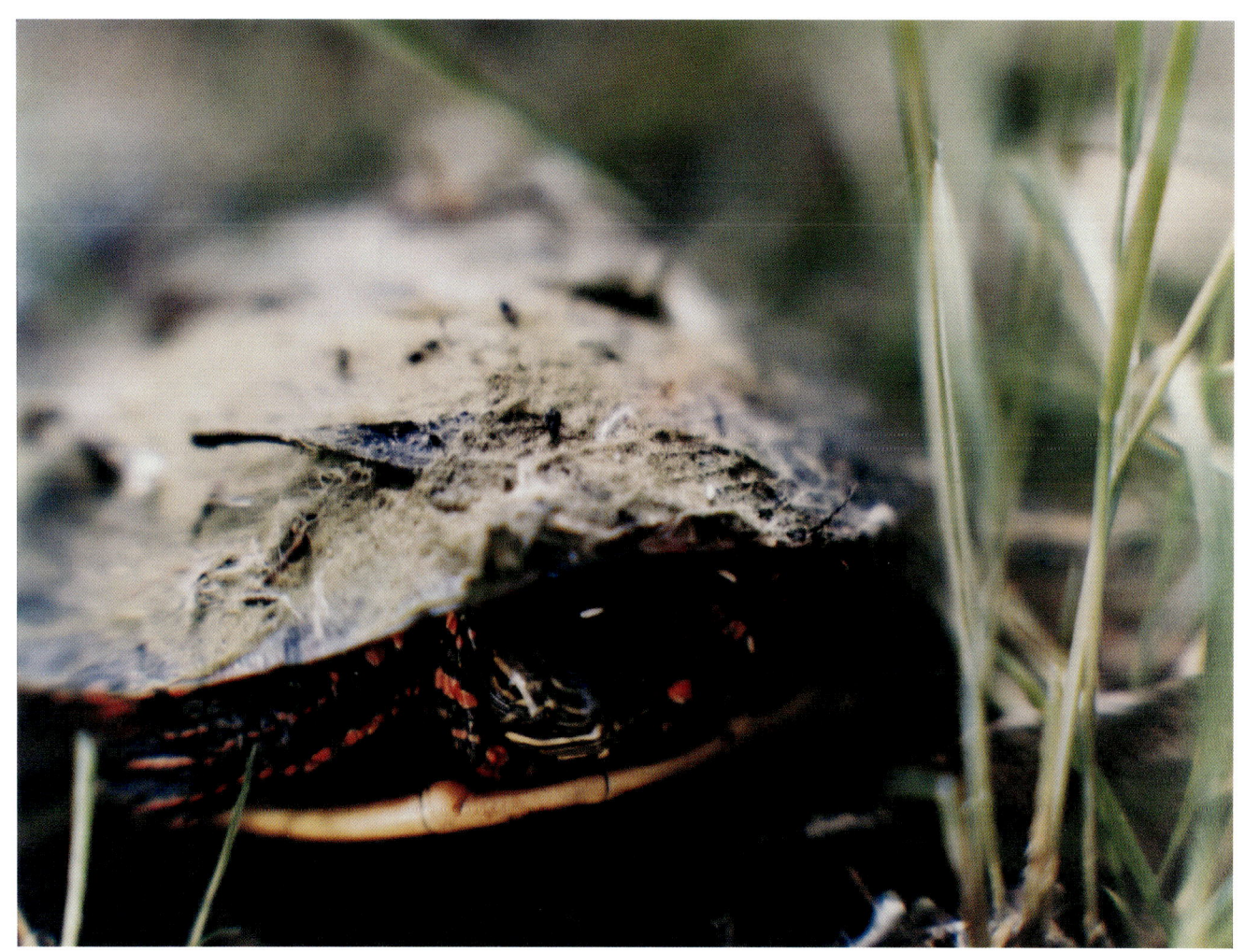

Painted Turtle

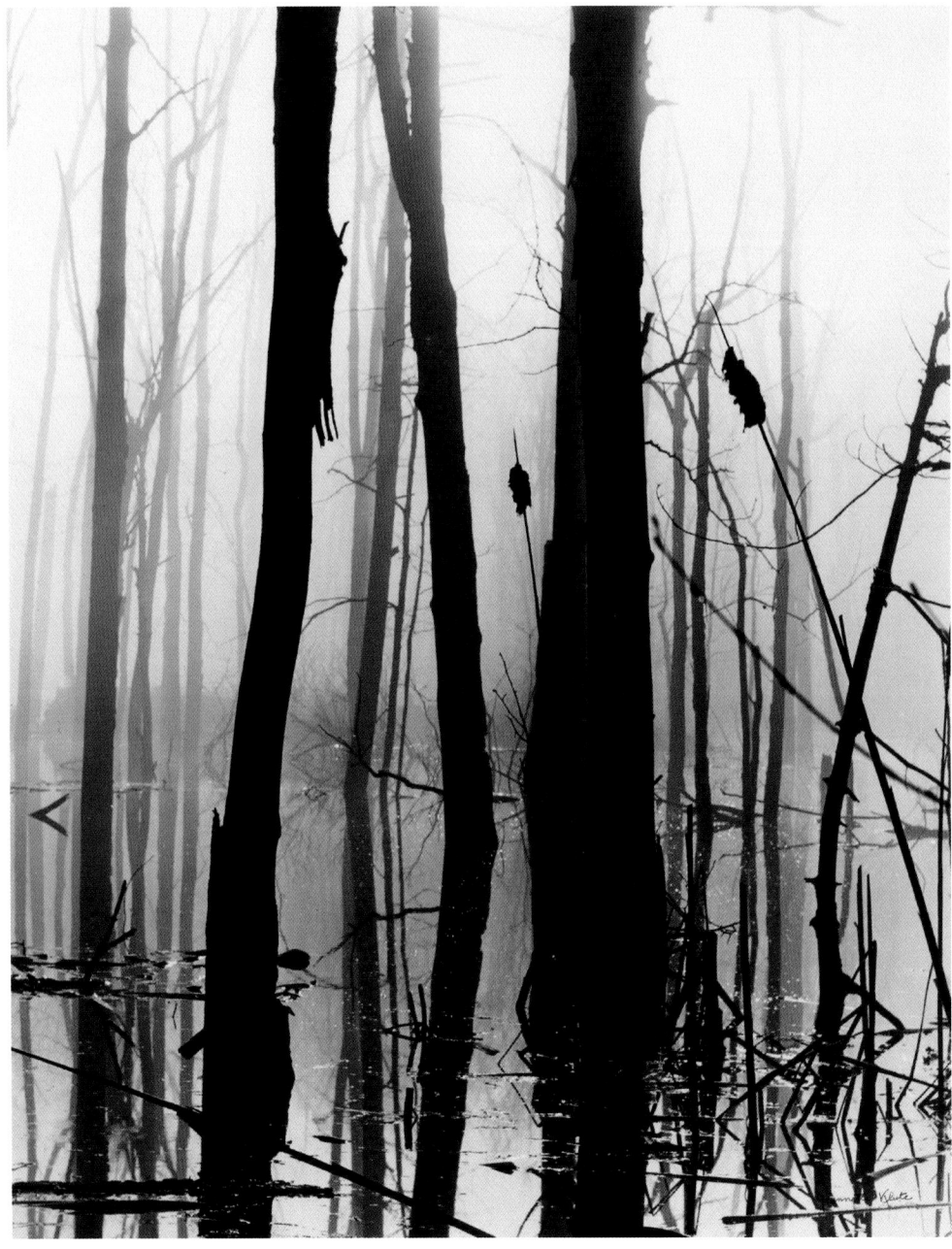

Trees in Winter

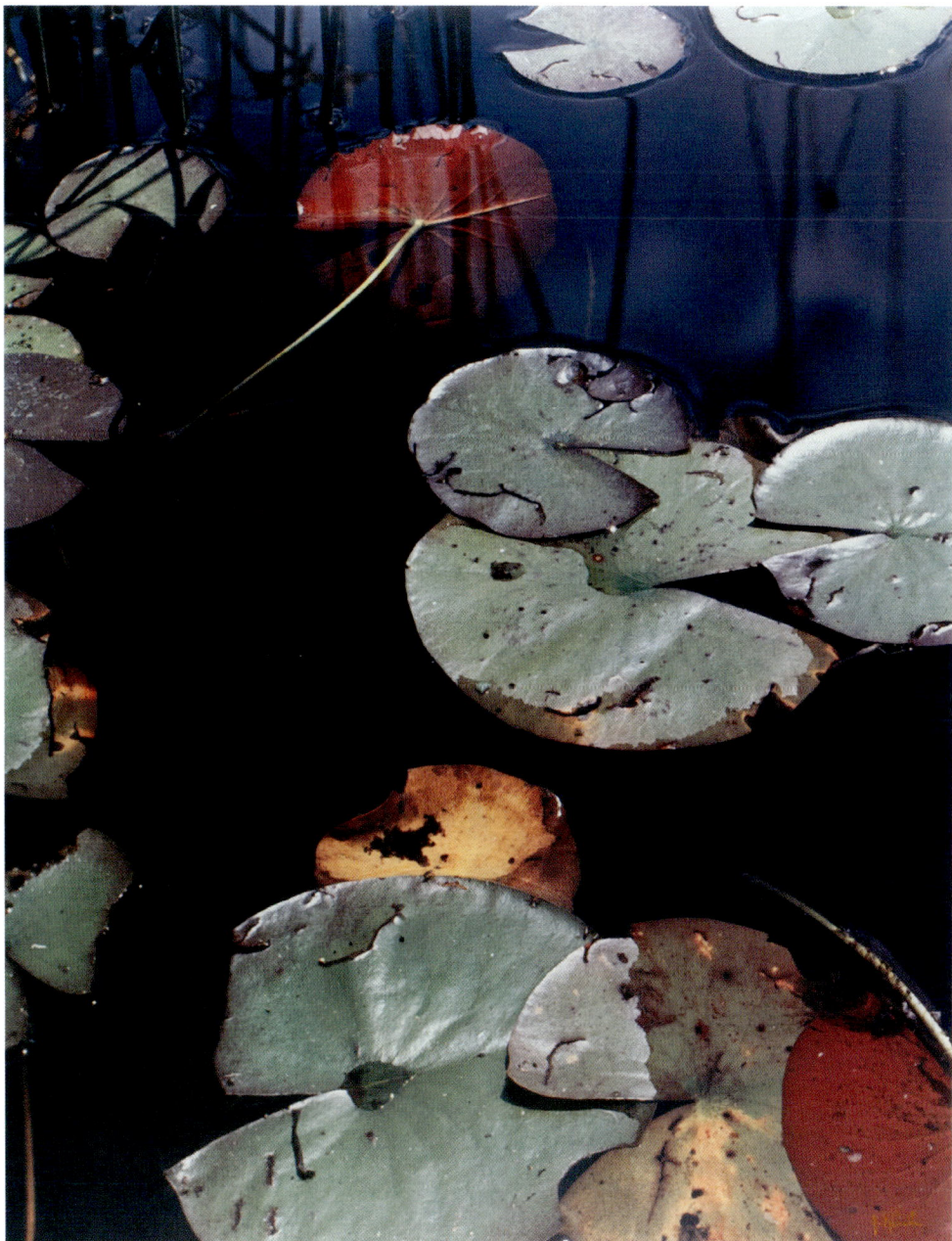

Lily Pads

51

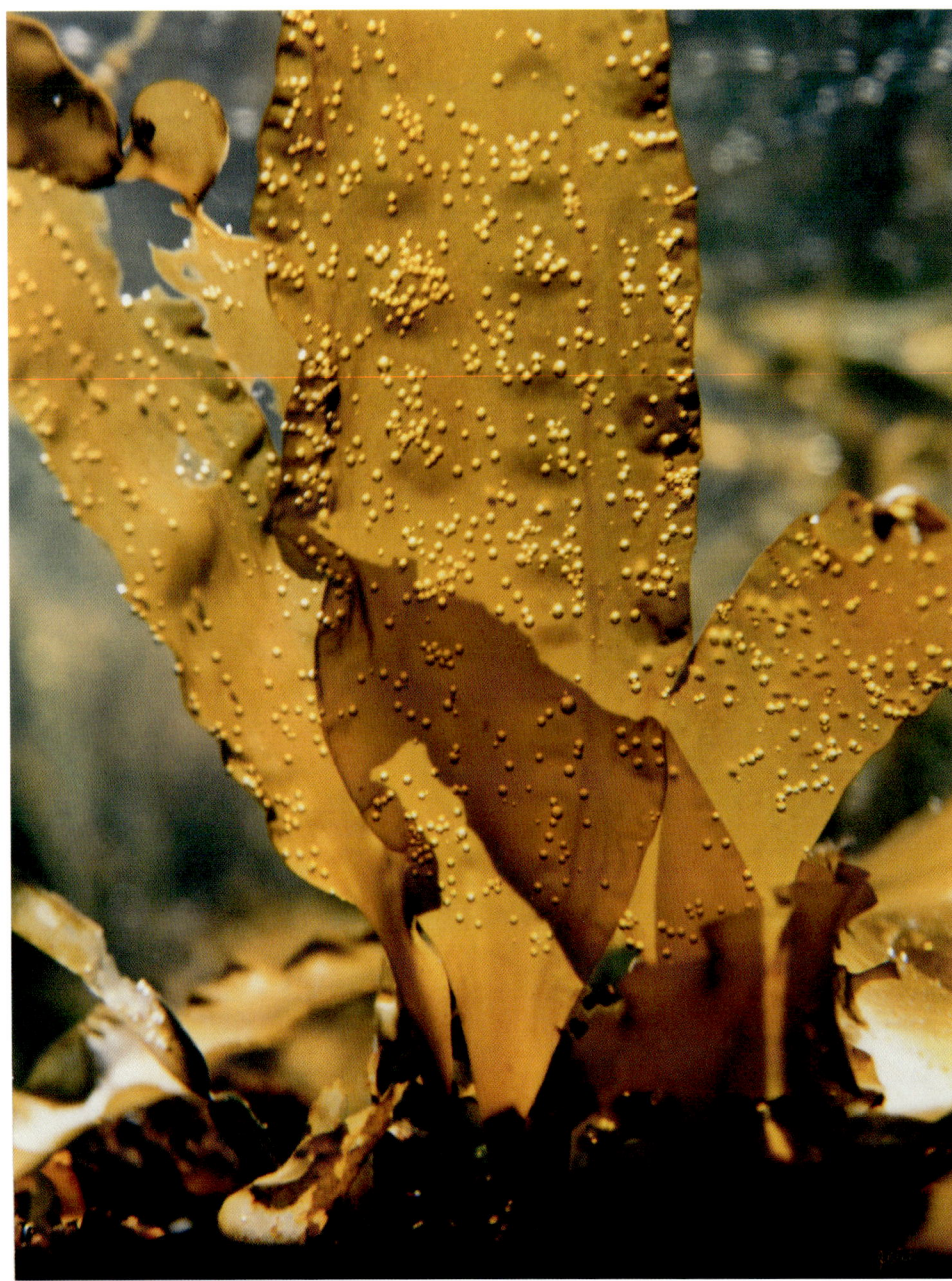

Yellow Kelp

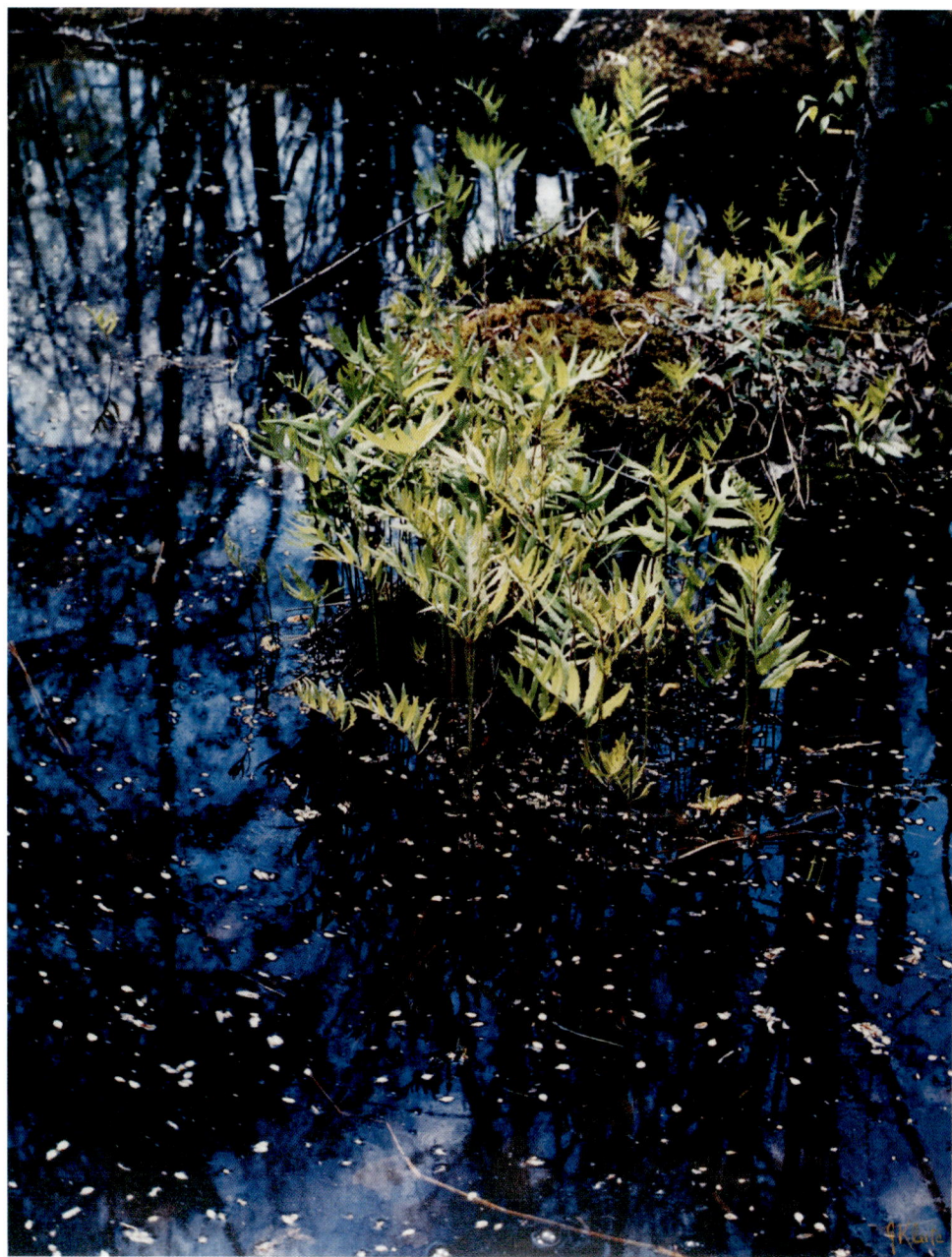

Sensitive Fern

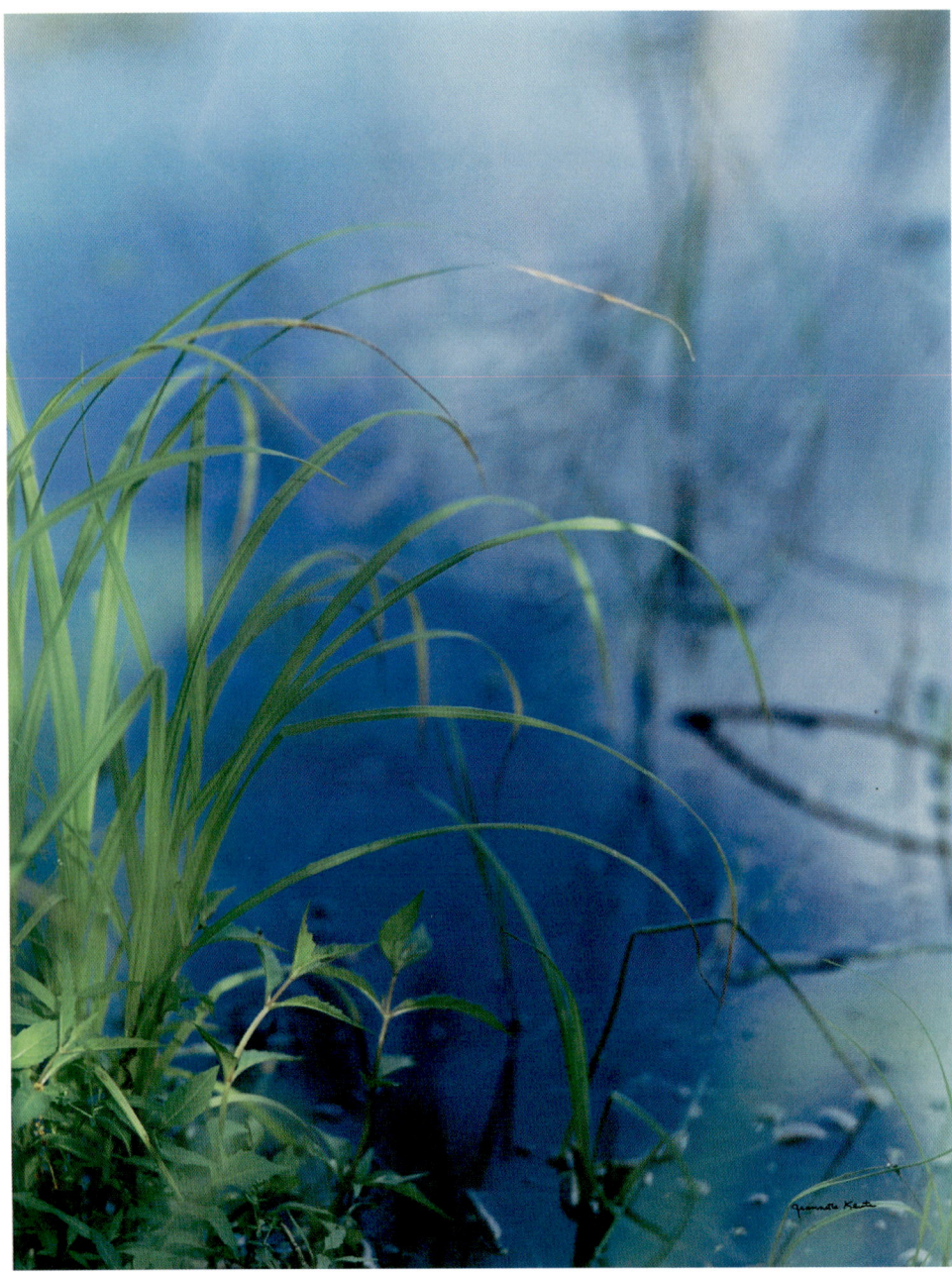

Blue Green

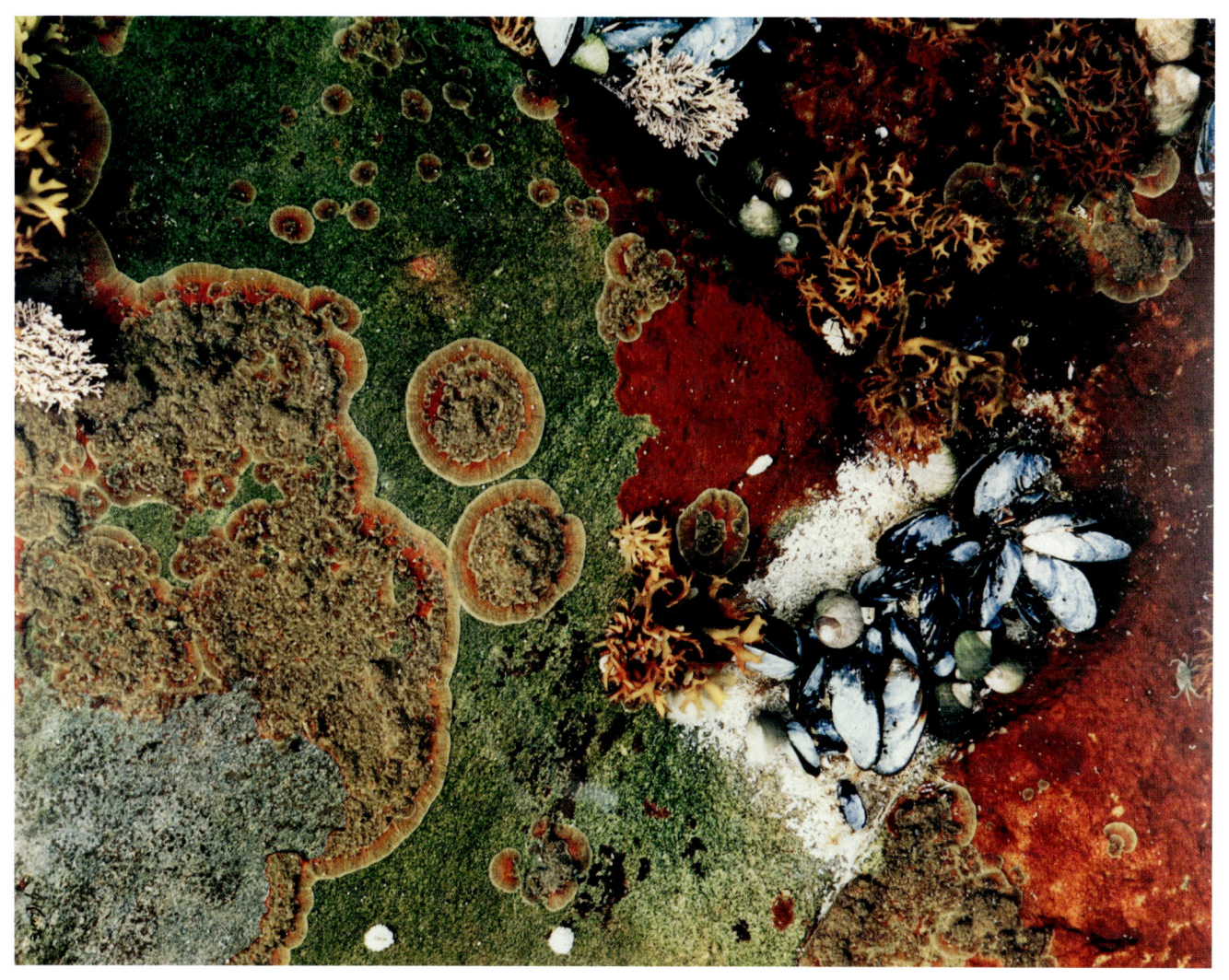

Mussels with Rust

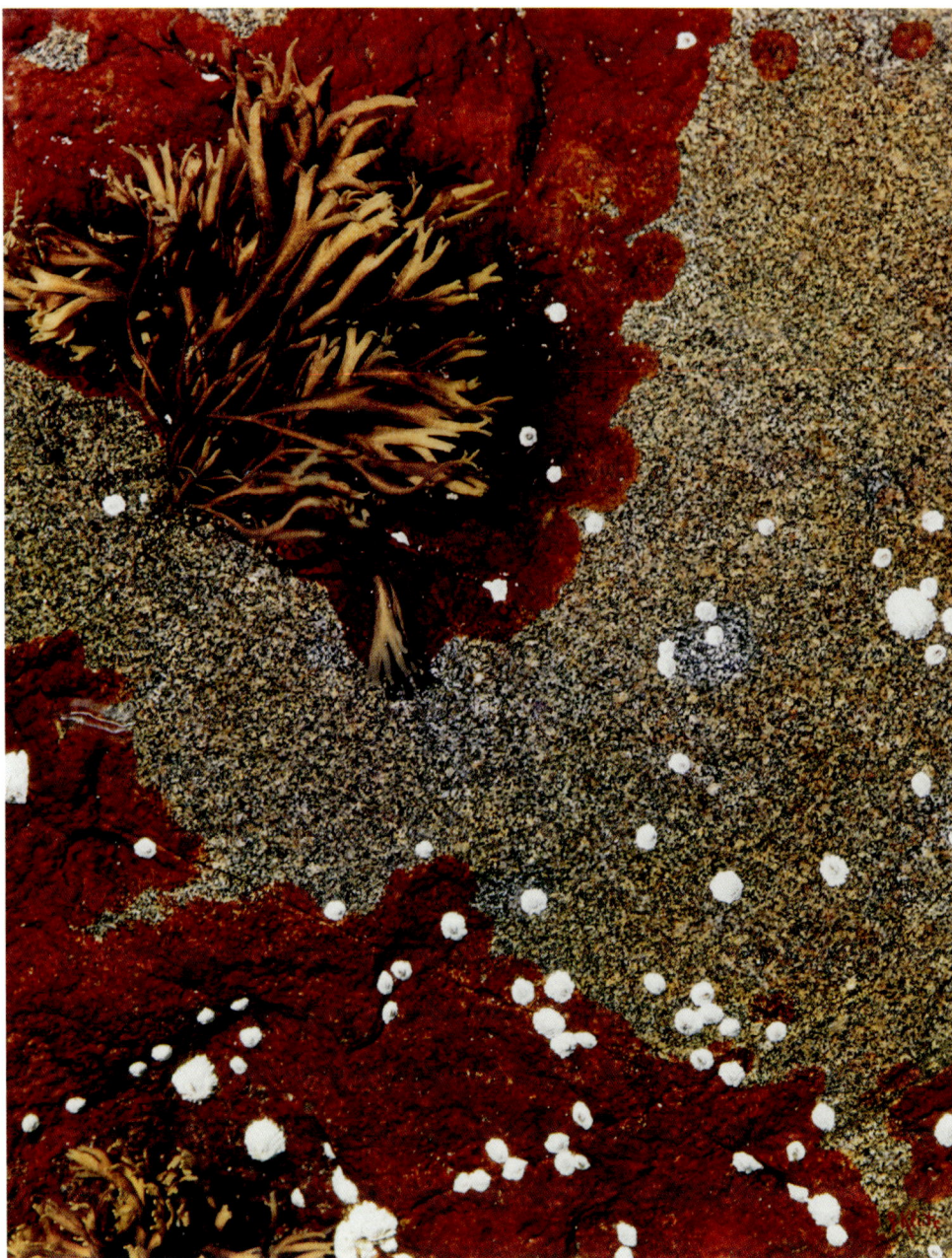

Gold and Rust

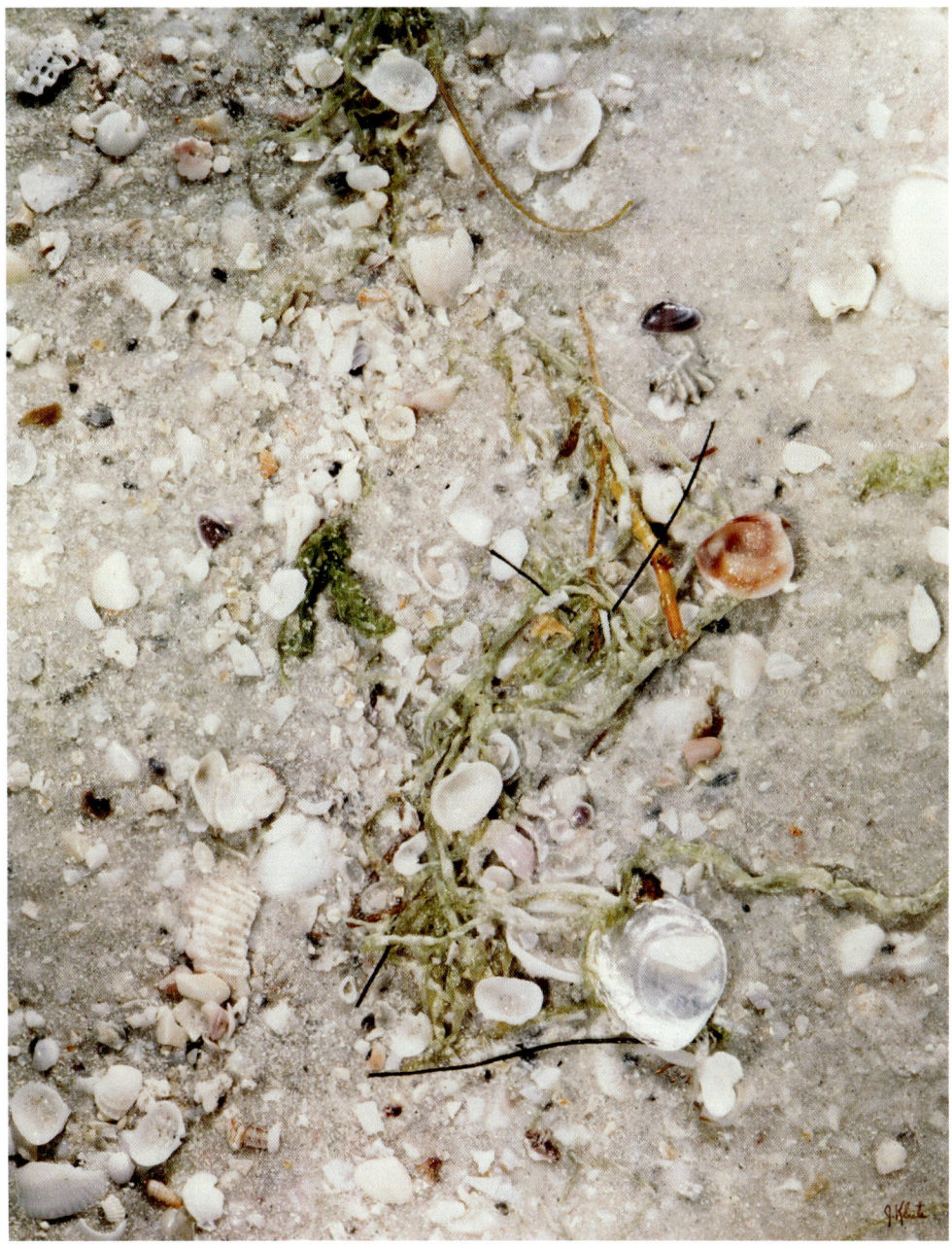

Florida Shells

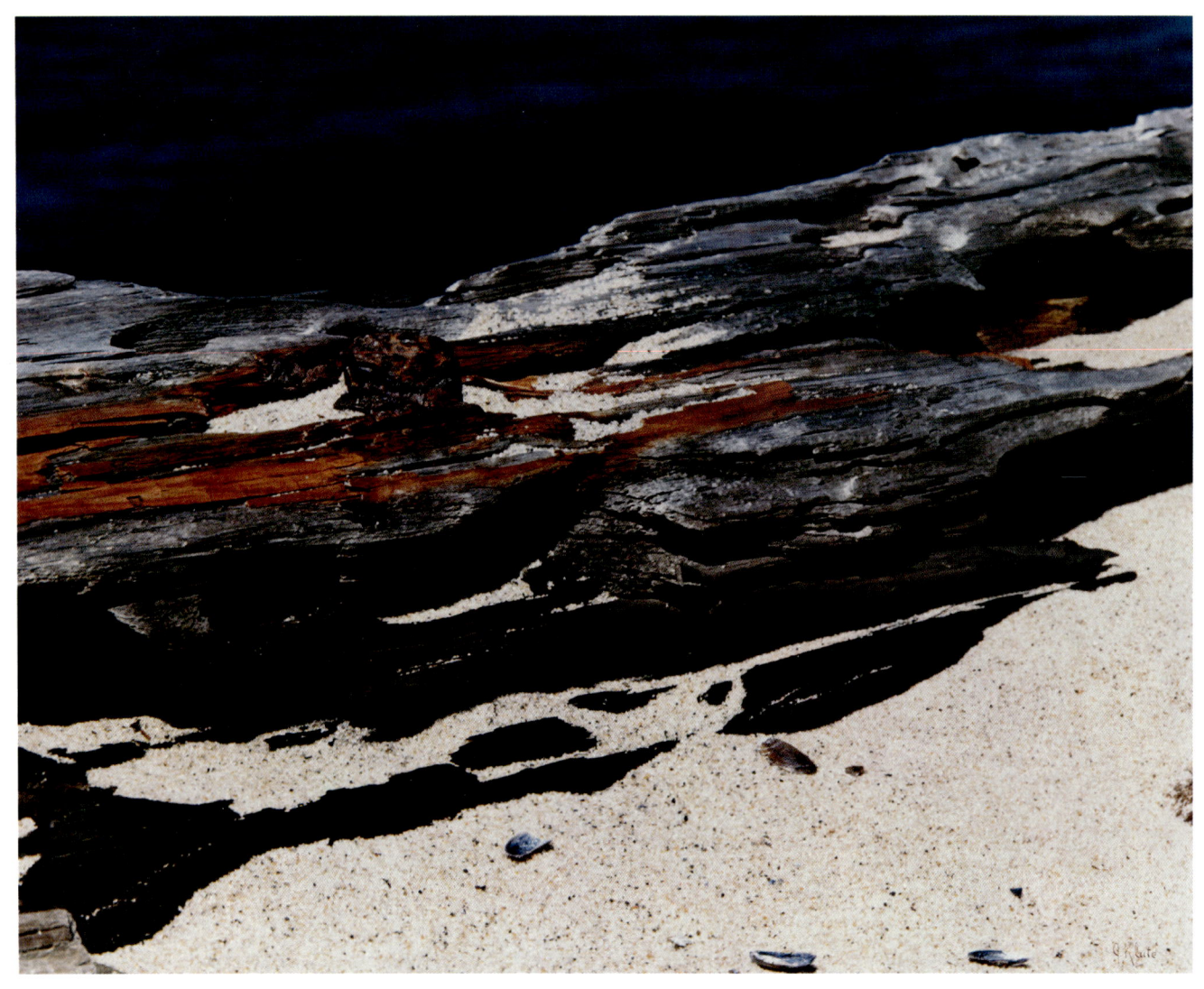

Weathered Log

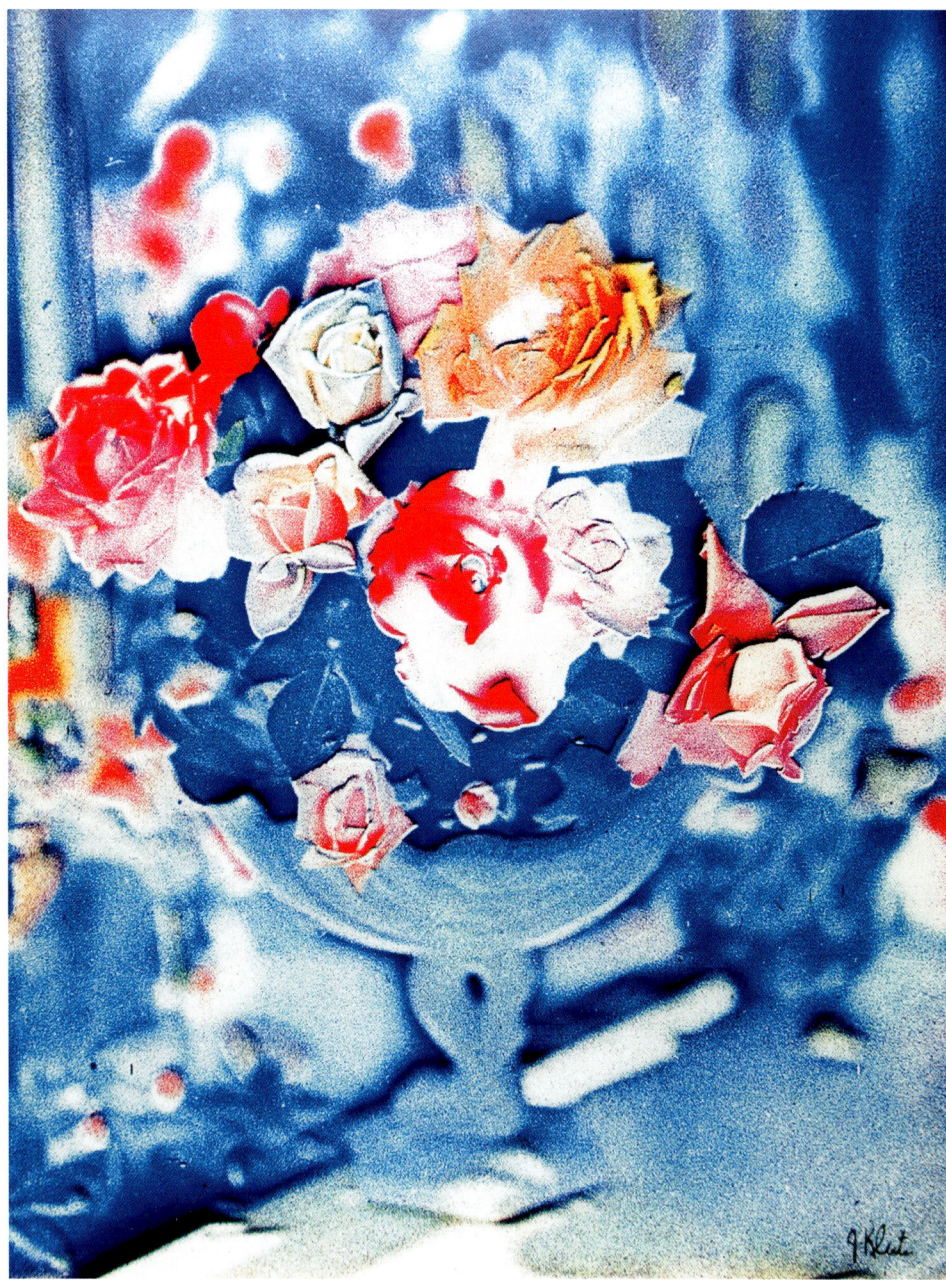

Derivation

59

Colophon

Design   Marnie Soom

Typeface   Electra and Caravan Ornaments, designed by William Addison Dwiggins

Paper   Endurance Silk

Printing   Global Printing, Alexandria, VA

This book was made possible, in part, through the generosity of Global Printing and, in part, by support from the RIT School of Photographic Arts and Sciences.